MW00332210

The Human Woman

THE HUMAN WOMAN

THE HUMAN WOMAN
BY LADY GROVE

You have awakened me to myself.

For that I thank you.

1888   1908.

LONDON: SMITH, ELDER AND CO.
15 WATERLOO PLACE.   MCMVIII

TO

MY HONOR

"*The two deepest characteristics of the new order are the scientific spirit and the democratic movement—a new conception of truth, and a new conception of authority and government.*"

"*Medievalism,*" by GEORGE TYRELL.

PREFACE

THE spirit in which the following pages
are offered to the public is not one in
which any claims are made for women, as
against men ; neither equality nor superiority, nor any quality the insistence upon
which tends to provoke the desire to controvert or to condemn, is made the basis of
what is hoped will be regarded as a sane
and temperate exposition of the views of
many women and perhaps more men.
The arguments in favour of extending the
franchise in any given direction being
perfectly familiar to all who have considered the political aspect of public affairs,
it has not been thought necessary to dwell
upon them in connection with the present
demand of duly qualified women to participate in the election of the representatives
of the "people." For, briefly, all the
reasons that have in the past been advanced
in favour of extending the franchise to men,

are applicable to women making the same demand. But the reasons for opposing this demand that have been put forward at any time, publicly or privately, by the great or by the obscure, by women or by men, have been patiently and conscientiously inquired into, during a period extending over nearly a quarter of a century, and as patiently and conscientiously dealt with in the matter contained in this book. Moreover, whereas so long as the question was considered "purely academic," and could be dismissed as "not being within the range of practical politics," the fact that women were not enfranchised did comparatively little harm ; but since the agitation has reached its present dimensions it has assumed different proportions, and there is a possibility of its becoming a grave menace to the welfare of the community. For there is a small but growing section of agitators who are working on wrong lines— they are inculcating, and ministering to the false idea of the antagonism of sex. They seek to vilify the best traditions of public life by trying to traduce the motives

PREFACE

of the ministers of the crown. And when the franchise is, as it inevitably must be, conceded to women, if this spirit be not presently checked—a spirit of shallow egotism totally distinct from enlightened self-interest—a new and warring element will be introduced into political life which the upholders of the Woman's Movement, in its best and highest aspects, not only earnestly deplore, but believe to be directly contrary to the aspirations and beliefs which gave birth to the movement.

In its true aspect the demand that women are making through their best representatives is a plea for the removal of the artificial man-made barriers, that exist to the detriment of the progress of the Anglo-Saxons as a nation, and of human beings as a race. It is a plea for women to be allowed free development for the faculties and functions they possess, not for permission to enter spheres for which they are by nature unfit. But let it be understood that we recognise the right of none to pronounce where these spheres lie. That shall be determined by the makers of

history present and future, and it is for
us humbly to acquiesce in the fate the
future has in store for us, and as humbly
to take our part in the moulding of that
future. I believe, with the conviction
born of many years of earnest study, that
the fate of a nation depends upon the
part played in it by the women of that
nation. I believe that the annihilation
that overtook the Egyptians, the Greeks,
and the Romans, would overtake this
still greater people, if the women failed
to take their share in its development,
as a nation. But happily such annihilation has been averted from us. The
few, the comparatively few, women who
have realised the impending danger have
made it impossible. The women who
have been aroused from whatever cause,
and with whatsoever motive, have been
the instrument whereby a great movement has been set on foot, and from
which there is no turning back. Gradually, one by one, and bit by bit, the
hindrances to the free development of
all the forces of the human mind will

crumble away. There will be no clean sweep, nothing will be swept away. Indeed, so gradually but so inevitably will the changes take place that the opposition at present existing will, when looked back upon, be regarded as the chimerical delusions of an obscured vision. This necessary upheaval towards a better state of things, without which every nation must sink into degradation and decay, is a stupendous force of which we are merely one of the instruments. How long it has been working silently and unobserved we cannot tell ; but we do know that in our day it has taken visible form, and that every person belonging to the movement is an essential part of the inevitable process of evolution. From the woman who sees in the end nothing but the probable amelioration of her own lot, often a by no means despicable or unworthy instrument ; from the man who when joining the movement sees no further, to the men and women who see in it the finger of God pointing to the destiny of the human race, and to the ultimate triumph of the

PREFACE

indwelling righteousness of humanity, all
are doing the work that must be done.
Meantime it is for us, the conscious active
individual workers, with plodding per-
tinacity, patiently to set forth our case as
best we may, to offer our poor little grain
of logic and of love to the glorious harvest
to be reaped hereafter ; to take our share
in weeding out the tares of cant, ignorance,
and oppression so surely and so speedily to
be overcome, and to be content to feel
that if one single prejudice be, through
us, removed, we have not worked in vain.

A. G.

51 BEDFORD SQUARE, LONDON,
September 1908.

NOTE.—I am indebted to the Editors of the *Nineteenth Century and After*, the *Fortnightly Review*,
the *Cornhill Magazine*, and others, for kind permission to reprint many of these essays, while some
of them appear for the first time in this volume.

CONTENTS

THE HUMAN WOMAN

I

THE THREE K'S

" Few now hold that the chief business of
women is the kitchen and the nursery ;
plain facts are against that odious and
ignoble view." This was the message the
most philosophical of living statesmen
sent on the 14th of March 1905 to the
meeting assembled in Queen's Hall in
support of the Parliamentary Bill to be
introduced that Session demanding the
removal of woman's legal disabilities.
" Few hold this odious and ignoble view."
But I venture gravely and respectfully to
ask Lord Morley to consider with me
whether, after all, this view need be so
very degrading ? Do we not all remember the famous utterance of the German
Emperor on the extent, or, as he imagines
it, the limit of woman's sphere ? With

A

unconscious humour, he enunciated a sentiment emulating the famous description of elementary education as consisting of the "Three R's." He limits, and imagines the limitation to be the narrowest, the sphere of women to "The three K's—*Kinder, Küche, Kirche;*" or rendered into English, "the three C's—children, cooking, and church." Now, far from desiring to stigmatise this view as odious and ignoble, I am prepared to agree with it, and feel inclined gently to lead the worthies who hold this view by the hand and patiently to point out to them that, unconsciously, their steps have wandered on to an exceeding high mountain : that they are veritably surveying all the kingdoms of the world, and the glory thereof ; are proclaiming the truth that no otherwhere than in these unbounded regions lies woman's sphere, and that it is only the petrifying blindness of self-satisfied egotism that prevents the recognition of this palpable fact.

The laws relating to "*lèse-majesté*" fortunately do not extend beyond the

Emperor's own dominions, otherwise it would be well to remember that

> A subject's faults a subject may proclaim,
> A monarch's errors are forbidden game.

This wise injunction was evidently disregarded by a certain traveller, of whom the story is told that he found himself tapped on the shoulder by a German constable in the streets of Berlin, and led away into custody for giving vent to the expression, "That d——d fool of an Emperor." "But," expostulated the unfortunate person under arrest, "it was not the *German* Emperor to whom I was referring." "Come, come, that won't do," the minion of the law is reported to have responded. "There is only *one* d——d fool of an Emperor, and that is ours!"

But I must elucidate the agreement I expressed with this pithy saying of the German Emperor's, not with that of his constable. Well, my accord with his Majesty rests on this view : that I should like any one to point out to me any matter in heaven above, or on the earth beneath,

or in the reputed region under the earth,
where one or other of these three subjects
does not enter. Let the existence of this
spot be clearly demonstrated to me, either
on earth or elsewhere, and then I relegate
that snug corner here, or still snugger
corner down below, with a sigh of relief
to—" men only."

Let us tackle these three C's cate-
gorically.

1. *Children.*—Where does *their* province
begin or end ? For not even the German
Emperor can by " children " mean only
our own individual offspring. When a
person knows *everything* appertaining to
the child—its birth, its life, its death,
its growth, its health, its mental, moral,
spiritual, and physical development, its
work, its play, its welfare as governed by
the State, its happiness as best furthered in
the home, what a colossal monument of
knowledge that person would be, and what
position would he, or she, not be fitted for ?

2. Then *Cooking.* Is this a limited
sphere ? The brain reels at the thought
of the number of subjects involved in a

comprehensive comprehension of everything connected with human food. Here
are a few connected with dietary, alimen-
tation, and gastronomy : therapeutics,
more especially the prophylactical branch
of this science, botany, zoology, miner-
alogy, dynamics, mathematics, and physics.
Trades, seasons, imports, exports, taxes,
tariffs (reformed or unregenerate), and
many other questions enter in ; and last,
but not least, if a popular belief is to be
credited, the temper of the male portion
of the human race.

3. And the *Church.* It cannot be
only our prayers, O Emperor ! to which
we are bidden to attend. That would
not exhaust the subject under the heading
" Church." No, we must try to be faith-
ful to our trust and to know what there
is to be known. We must try to emulate
Mr. Gladstone's monumental research
into the origin, methods, and responsibilities of the Church in all ages. We
must endeavour " thoroughly to com-
prehend the eternal principles of the
commutation of the tithe rent-charge, and

the difference in the justice due to a transitory and a permanent curate"; possess "a double grasp of leading principle and intricate detail, an equal command of legal and historic controversy, and of all the actuarial niceties and puzzles of commutation!" Women should be alive to the "perils of Erastianism to the spiritual life of the Church; discern the advantages or disadvantages of disestablishment to the same end; broadly recognise the inevitable relation of Church and State; and be eager and able to read the signs of the times as to the prospects of Anglican, Catholic, or Lutheran Christianity." "The origin of simony, the validity of the Apostolic Succession and other matters, abstruse or simple," they should have a thorough mastery of, and "avoid all levity, precipitancy, or shallowness of mind in dealing with such subjects." Yes, all this and more is needed for a comprehensive understanding of the "Church."

This is not, it will be conceded, the unskilled work of the world, to be left

6

to women on account of their incompetence for higher things. No ; if women
would accept their responsibility in the regions of religion, the care of children, and
the feeding of the race, set themselves to
learn their tasks, and carry them out in a
practical way, on an economically sound
basis, the world's work would be revolu-
tionised and the world itself become " on
earth as it is in heaven."

Not content with accepting these
three great responsibilities, the German
Empress is said to have timidly pleaded
for the admission of a fourth K (*Kleider*).
For us another C (Clothing). And, indeed, I cannot imagine how the Emperor
so forgot himself as to omit so important
an adjunct to woman's modesty. For
who can doubt that it was to inculcate
modesty, and a becoming conception of
" their proper place," that he threw out
these words of wisdom to his country-
women. Perhaps, however, he knew
of the little girl who thrilled her
hearers with her accounts of her own
modesty, which she urged was so scrupu-

lous, that when occasion led her to
her looking-glass in order to see how
to fasten her brooch she invariably shut
her eyes.   In the same way his Imperial
Majesty no doubt thought that women
should clothe themselves, not only remem-
bering to forget what they clothed, but
how, when, and where the clothing where-
withal they arrayed themselves came into
existence If, moreover, the whole responsibility for the world's clothing be another
burden added to women's shoulders, we
can understand their " shirking their responsibility."   But we exempt the Emperor himself from having formulated this
fourth K, and can only regard the plea
for its inclusion as an instance of one of
those extravagances to which we all
know women are sometimes prone.

But so far from limiting women's
sphere, is not responsibility for even the
three K's asking rather too much of
them ? Sympathy will be felt with the
little village boy whose industry has
pushed him to the head of his school,
and who, on hearing the duties involved

8

by his headship solemnly enumerated by the schoolmaster, faltered out, " Please, sir, need I be head boy ? " " Please, sir, need I be a woman ? " some of us will feel inclined to petition whomsoever has the ordering of such matters, if the German Emperor's dictum is to be firmly insisted upon and conscientiously carried out.

" Ay, there's the rub ! " " Be a woman ! " is an injunction too seldom uttered and too seldom followed. " Be a man ! " is an exhortation familiar enough from the nursery to the battlefield, addressed by men and by women to boys and to men, and sometimes by men to themselves. There is a story of a foxhunting parson who came of a famous sporting family, and who, when approaching a formidable fence in the heat of the chase, was heard admonishing himself, " Be a man, Tom Fox, be a man ! " Say to each one of yourselves, my sisters, " Be a woman—be a woman." The task is not so easy nor so simple as some think, neither can its successful execution be overrated or its highest ideal reached.

II

THE IDEALS OF A WOMAN'S PARTY

In the last chapter I dealt with the German Emperor's dictum on the sphere of women, which he maintained was embraced by their adherence to the departments of life comprised in three German K's—children, cooking, and church, and in which, moreover, if he were willing to include a fourth K— clothes—I expressed myself as unable to disagree with him. Or, to put it more graciously, I was anxious to show my agreement with his Imperial Majesty in a manner that he had possibly not contemplated. From Majestic Imperialism, or perhaps I should say from Imperialistic Majesticism, the drop to even so renowned a periodical as the *Spectator* is a grave descent, and for the arguments of both I hope to provide a decent grave.

A WOMAN'S PARTY

In February this year the *Spectator* indulged in a take-it-or-leave-it piece of grandiloquent advice to the " thousands of good, quiet women " of this country " who believe that the proper sphere of the sex lies in directions very different from those which are approved of by the Woman's Suffrage Party." There is no sentence in any part of the article to indicate that the writer had taken steps to ascertain what are the ideals approved of by the " Woman's Suffrage Party." He has gleaned his knowledge, based his judgment, and uttered his condemnation on sensational paragraphs in the daily papers. The " spade work " of a hundred years is either unknown or ignored. " The silly behaviour of some of the leaders of the movement " is, he considers, " the best comment on their claims." When they " state in the police courts that they speak for the women of England, steps should be taken to challenge this statement." What, in the eyes of the *Spectator* (the newspaper, not the " man in the street "), constitutes leadership, we are entitled to ask, and who deputed the *Spectator* to nominate for us our leaders ? Because it suits certain of our opponents to try and belittle our movement, are the real leaders thereof thus easily to be dismissed and ignored ? Is the work that has been done for several generations ; are the sayings of John Stuart Mill, the greatest thinker of modern times ; is the lofty, noble championship of some of the best men and women that ever lived, to be thus set aside, because either through insufficient pains to acquire knowledge or an inadequate appreciation of honesty as the essential qualification of an educator, or both, the enemies of the movement choose to forget their existence ?

What, in truth, are the ideals of the woman's party as I understand it, and as it already stands, requiring, as I think, no " regeneration " so far as the loftiness of its aim is concerned ? That women should be allowed to work hand in hand with men, and to help directly in the beneficent work of reforming legislation.

A WOMAN'S PARTY

Why is it that, whenever it is a question
of men entering public life, the ideals
held out are those of self-sacrifice, attention to duty, disinterested concern for
the welfare of others, and a wise dis-
cretion in weighing the comparative
merits of different measures ?   When it
is a question of women taking an interest
in the same things, we hear from opponents of nothing but the demoralising
influence of the " hustings " (even though
they happen, in fact, no longer to exist !),
of the sordid atmosphere of political life,
of its meanness, its pettiness, the un-
worthiness of the motives that govern
public men, and the generally degrading
effect that " politics " have on those
participating in them.   But it is not
too much to say that the reforms that
have been most insistently urged, the
reforms that bear upon the home life
of the workers—the housing question,
the care of infant life, the temperance
movement—in a word, all the reforms
dealing particularly with " the home "
—are a by-product of the woman's

movement; that the women whose help and advice are sought, whose opinions are acted upon, are all and every one of them in favour, and strongly in favour, of the enfranchisement of their own sex.

In Australia, where the vote is an established fact, the ideals of the woman's party aim essentially at the improvement of the home, not at the demoralisation or "the desertion of the home for the hustings," as the cant phrase has it. In New South Wales women have had the vote only since August 1902, and in less than four years they have won reforms which the voteless women of Victoria have asked for for fifteen years, and are still asking for in vain. These reforms deal one and all with the purification of the home.

This cannot be insisted upon too often and too earnestly. They deal with the protection of child-life in more than one way: by the establishment of a children's court; by an Habitual Criminal Act; by the licensing of juvenile street vendors; by the prohibition of the sale

of intoxicating drinks and indecent literature to children ; by the legitimisation
of children on the marriage of parents,
thus giving them a fairer start in life,
and remedying, as far as it lies in the
power of the State to do so, the wrong
done them by their parents ; by the
raising of the " age of consent " to seven-
teen years ; and by other reforms which
it would take too long to enumerate,
but which include the limiting of the
hours of child-labour, and an improvement in the conditions under which
children work. "The home" is safe-
guarded, exalted, and made more real
in every way in which State interference
can make such an improvement possible.
And the improvement is even greater
indirectly than it can be made by direct
legislation, *because* of the loftiness of the
ideals aimed at.

The English women who prate about
" the home " apparently care little that
the homes of their poorer sisters should
in some cases be a mere mockery of
the name, and only approximate in the

faintest degree to a resemblance of their
own snug dwellings. I solemnly affirm
that it is a belief in the sanctity of the
home, and a desire to make it a national
reality, instead of the catchword of the
prosperous, that causes women to emerge
from their homes and bear the obloquy
and resentment of the "thousands of
good and quiet women," whose goodness
consists chiefly in the flinging of self-
righteous but anonymous stones at the
courageous few who brave insult and
ridicule in discharge of what they believe
to be a sacred duty : whose "quiet"
virtues do not sink to the level of every
day's most common need, but remain in
the tepid regions of selfish contentment
in which it has pleased circumstance to
call them.

I am not referring only to the comparatively recent exhibitions of courage
and self-sacrifice, which have been a
target for the world's arrows. However
mistaken some of us may think their
methods, let us at least give credit for
sincerity of motive and singleness of aim

16

to those whose inspiration leads them to take a different view of the road to success than others of us who are determined to reach the same goal are travelling by. The early pioneers of the movement also braved insult and ridicule in maintaining their belief in the need for women's co-operation in public affairs. Cowards fear usurpation where brave men welcome enlightened co-operation in what I am willing to believe both regard as a high and noble duty.

And surely, as far as woman's own fears are concerned, surely the fear of pollution is more degrading than a brave determination to face the facts of life as they are ; a brave determination to share the burden of responsibility with those who are honestly trying to help forward the progress of the world ; a brave determination to use the powers they possess in a womanly striving to better their own and other people's conditions, to help to ameliorate the unhappiness caused by poverty, ignorance, and crime.

THE HUMAN WOMAN

To those who are and ever have been surrounded by the gentle atmosphere of opulent well-being, I admit that it requires intelligence and imagination, as well as courage, to *see* the necessity for the abandonment of the sluggish ideals of a barren self-sufficiency. Their attitude of mind is not the outcome of the refining influence of cultivated leisure, as they would have us believe, for this influence would make women acquainted with the world's need, and ashamed of shirking their share of responsibility, instead of self-complacently hugging their incapacity. The vaunted refinement of the anti-suffragists is "a hollow sham, disguising the coarse supremacy of wealth."

And *it is not true* that women can do all that is required of them by God and man in their present condition. The voice that has called some of them to abandon the old ideals (if ideals they can be called) in favour of more active participation in the world's work is the voice of the Eternal dwelling in the hearts of men, calling them to buckle on the armour of

18

sympathy and understanding, and to shirk
nothing that these attributes involve.

Is this hypocrisy or " hysteria " ? Are
these mere words ? Let those ready and
willing to fling this taunt beware lest their
unawakened souls be found guilty of the
one unpardonable sin.

For how is the line to be drawn or the
distinction to be made between the advisability of woman voting for the representatives of, and being themselves eligible for
election on all municipal bodies, and in the
advisability of their being allowed the vote
for members of the Imperial Parliament ?
What has the passing of the Local Authorities Qualification of Women's Act done ?
It has enabled electors to place directly
elected women on education authorities,
and to secure their services in other
matters of local government, such as the
housing of the poor, the looking after
public lodging-houses, the management
of the female side of lunatic asylums, the
regulation of the employment of women,
provision for the prevention of cruelty
to children, the supervision of industrial

schools (containing children from three years of age), the supervision of mid-wives, and of baby-farmers, of homes for inebriate women, of police courts and police court waiting-rooms, and generally to secure their co-operation in matters relating to public health.

These are the womanly offices that women asked to be allowed to fill, and their demands were greeted with howls of execration in both Houses of Parliament. I listened to some of the howls of execration myself in the House of Lords, and I heard Lord James of Hereford solemnly warn their Lordships that, if this demand were conceded to women, there would not be a shadow or a tittle of ground whereon to deny them the Parliamentary vote. It was the only phrase and the only sentiment in the speech with which I found myself in agreement, but of the irresistible logic of his contention there can be no doubt.

These are the sane, profitable, and essentially womanly ideals involving, to my mind, the obligation on the part of woman to recognise her concern in all the affairs of the State from the meanest parochial matter to the highest Imperial interests—ideals that, in one or other of their aspects, the workers in this movement have ever held before their own and their followers' eyes. Yet that deliberate attempts are made to ignore the real foundation upon which this gigantic structure is built, by those undertaking to instruct on the subject, the following paragraph will show :—

" Women who have made a serious study of economic problems, or who have felt instinctively that their sphere is the home and not the hustings, may have been inclined hitherto to dismiss as unimportant the more violent fatuities of the suffrage party. They may have considered that female politicians who chain themselves to railings or deliberately court physical conflict with policemen are better left to the prison-cell or the asylum. *But if the movement started by such persons* develops into a campaign, which is not merely foolish but dangerous, they may well decide that the time has arrived for more positive action than silent contempt."

The writing of the words I have italicised is an example of what I have referred to as want of knowledge or contempt for honesty. If the assertion be the outcome of the former, what possible weight can the views of a journal lending itself to such unfortunate tactics carry in the minds of thousands of intelligent beings who look for enlightenment from the pages of the *Spectator*? If prompted by the latter, whom does it attempt to deceive? This ostrich-like policy of trying to ignore the solidity and solidarity of a movement that is surging through almost every civilised country in the world, is neither wise, nor virtuous, nor even " respectable." Therefore, it passes the wit of man why it should be adopted by the *Spectator*.

But it is not only in dealing with the alleged insignificance of the movement that facts are misrepresented, which is the description the courtesies of controversy force us to give to the mis-statements contained in the article I am alluding to, but the very significance of the movement is purposely perverted.

"The wife of a man who is unable to find employment can think little of joy or peace if she is not sure that she can keep a roof above her head, or find bread for her children. When, therefore, she, in her doubt and unhappiness, is actually assured that the cause of her distress is due to her political disabilities ; when she is informed that *her remedy lies in giving the balance of political power to women instead of men*—when such perilous stuff as that is offered by the ignorant and the hysterical as food for the hungry, then it is time for women who can think clearly and speak soberly to set to work, and to strengthen their work with a pledge of comradeship."

Can the writer of the above accusation quote one single utterance of any responsible or even irresponsible leader of the movement to justify the assumption that the cause for women's suffrage is represented as a desire to give the balance of political power to women instead of to

men ? That with the establishment of
this state of things, and not before, will
there be a possibility of the vote having a
beneficial effect on the laws that govern
the condition of women as workers ? If
not, I deliberately bring the gravest charge
that can be brought against any journalist
—that of purposely purveying false information to his readers in order to damage
a cause towards which he is personally
antagonistic.

It is suggested that " there is a need for
the formation of a woman's party pledged,
not to obtain the Parliamentary vote, but
to the essential woman's work of regeneration of the ideals and influences of home
life in the best and widest sense of the
words." " It is true," adds the writer,
with the cautious reflection that women's
universal nobility and devotion to an ideal
are going to be made in a later portion
of the same article the basis of what
will be shown to be a futile argument,
" it is true that for most women there is
no need for such a pledge." It is for
the "regeneration" of the small minority

of misguided women who have allowed themselves to take an interest in other concerns than those contained within their own walls and those of their limited circle of friends that this new missionary work is to be undertaken. We are to be taught that "love, joy, peace, long-suffering, gentleness, goodness, faith, meekness" (especially meekness), "and temperance" are the ideals of life "for women only." Men, we presume, with that characteristic bearing of the burdens of life, have forsworn all these delectable qualities (or most of them), because they and the exercise of a vote cannot go together. Anyhow, not in women. Let them once presume to record a vote or listen to the shocking tales that will be poured into their ears in order to induce them to bestow their suffrages on one or other of the lovelorn, joyless, war-like, impatient, violent, evil, faithless, arrogant, intemperate possessors of a vote and lo ! their golden chariots will become pumpkins, their prancing steeds mere whisking mice, and the pearls and diamonds of their speech turned to the vomiting of toads and snails !

"It is one of the commonplaces of practical politics that it is necessary from time to time to state and restate in the plainest possible language what a thing is, and the reason why it is what it is. It may seem superfluous to do so ; the facts and the reasons may be so patent that to state them once more may seem as foolish as to walk about repeating the alphabet, or insisting that two and two make four. The reply must be that large numbers of people are always forgetting the alphabet, or trying to prove that two and two make five. *It is evidently necessary*, in the present instance, to state once more *the plain reason why women cannot have the Parliamentary vote ; cannot, that is, take a deciding part in framing the legislation of the State.* It is not because they are inferior to men in morals, in courage, in patriotism, or in intellectual power. In heart and head the sexes are equal. But it is because women are inferior to men in physical strength. It is a very old reason, but most things that are true are very old."

It may be interesting to note that this simple illustration from arithmetic has been anticipated by Mr. Israel Zangwill in language of which the words I have just quoted sound strangely like an echo.

"Our case," said Mr. Zangwill, just a year ago, "is so simple, that it is like having to prove that one and one are two Indeed, this is precisely what the opposition denies. It says that one and one are not two ; that in politics one man and one woman are only one, and man is that one. Savages are notoriously bad at arithmetic, but in the Colenso of civilisation it is written that one man and one woman are two persons. Like most simple truths, this axiom of spiritual arithmetic has taken the human race a long time to arrive at ; but, thank Heaven, we are there at last ! Woman is a separate and individual personality ; a human soul, and, what is more to the point, a tax-payer. Even marriage cannot extinguish her. She is no longer a mere ap-

pendage to her lord, united and fused. The
Married Woman's Property Act gives her
the right to her separate property ; with
property goes taxation, and with taxation
must and shall go representation."

The latest adopter of this dazzling
example of mathematical accuracy seems to
think its demonstration as an argument quite
final and conclusive. I suggest as a para-
phrase to this "unanswerable argument"—

"You cannot *have* a vote, my dear.
Haven't you heard me say so ? If you
want to know why, which is ridiculous
after the firm way I have been talking,
why then it's because you are my inferior
—in physical strength. Now you know.
Your brain is as good as mine—at least,
those of you who do not clamour for a
vote (No woman asks quietly for it, and
if she does I don't hear her.) Your heart
and morals are perhaps better, the difference in your courage and patriotism could
hardly be detected, but because you are,
or I think and choose to say you are,
weaker than I am, therefore I will keep
the one thing to myself that you perhaps
stand most in need of.'

But is the writer afraid of urging this paradox to its illogical conclusion ? Not he ! The following remarks are made without the smallest indication that the writer is otherwise than solemnly in earnest :—

" If women had the Parliamentary Suffrage, there might, nay, almost certainly would, come a time when the one sex, as a whole, found itself in sharp conflict with the other sex on some momentous social problem, and the result would be worse than deplorable, it would be terrible. It would be anarchy in its most disintegrating and dreadful form. For, remember, the last resort of the sharpest political disagreement is always the same. It was the resort of the English citizens who dethroned Charles I. ; it was the resort of the States of the North when the Confederacy strove to dissolve the Union ; it was the weapon well-nigh drawn from the scabbard before the reforms of 1832 ; and it is a weapon which women could never draw with the faintest hope of success. Is that exaggeration ? Is the idea of personal conflict between men and women incredible or impossible ? Let us put a particular case. Suppose that in the House of Commons women were actually represented by the majority of members, because there were more women on the registers than men. Suppose that a Bill were introduced to curtail the power of the liquor trade to an extent immensely in advance of the reform desired by the majority of male opinion. If the Bill became law, and the great majority of the men refused to obey it, what would happen ? The women could not enforce the law they had made, because they could not command the police or the arsenals. The situation would be ridiculous until, with the attempt to enforce the law, it became horrible. The supreme irony of the struggle would be that woman's very nobility and devotion to an ideal would drive her to the bitterest end. The word ' compromise ' for her could not exist ; she would insist upon a decision, even though she knew that she must go under in upholding her belief."

After this lengthy quotation, the article

extends to another half-column of the *Spectator*, but what need we further witness? I have dealt elsewhere with the impossibility of knowing whether "women were actually represented by a majority of members." The ballot is in itself a complete answer to this "argument." But what insidious poison is there in a Parliamentary vote that could cause the exhibition of a phenomenon never hitherto observed? "There *certainly would*," says our prophet, "come a time when the one sex, *as a whole*, found itself in sharp conflict with the other sex on some momentous social problem." Is this exaggeration? he exclaims. Is the idea of personal conflict between the sexes incredible or impossible? "Let us put a particular case." On getting thus far I shut my eyes and mentally marshalled all my reason to my aid. Here with my eyes I was to receive the fatal revelation that should bring my faith tottering to the ground. What was the prospect, "free from all exaggeration," "not only possible, but certain," that was unfolded

before my horror-stricken mental vision ?
Every woman in all the British Isles
drawn up in battle array against all the
men — fighting — and for what ? The
curtailing of the liquor trade. Think of
it. Who dares say that drunkenness is
on the increase among women ? We
know, for the *Spectator* has told us so, that
the vote in woman's hands would change
all that. Whatever her proclivities, we
know that the whole of womankind, " for
whom compromise does not exist," and on
account of her nobility and devotion to
an ideal, would " go solid " for a Bill
" immensely in advance " of anything that
men have ever contemplated or ever could
or ever would contemplate. Where are
all the men's temperance bodies ? Where
are the so-called fanatical temperance
leaders ? Gone, alas ! driven to drink by
voting women. Where, too, would be
the women whose very existence depends
upon the liquor traffic ? The barmaids
(who so vigorously and successfully de-
fended the attempt to abolish them as a
class), the wives and daughters of publicans,

the wives and daughters of brewers, the
widows whose sole means of subsistence
is derived from the trade ?   All united as
women, though it should involve their
extinction as human beings united, in defence of an "ideal" against the brutal male !
"The situation would be ridiculous" (Oh,
surely not !) "until with the attempt to
enforce the law it became horrible."

Do even women display such self-
destructive quixotism ?   It is not an
attempt to construct a bogey out of
woman's high and noble attributes ?
Whereas in truth no quality has a sex and
no sex has the monopoly of any quality.

But let us examine this dogmatic assertion that "war is the *ultima ratio*."   It
is accompanied by the glib assumption,
which is apparently regarded as an indisputable axiom, that "Nature has deprived
women of the right to use that argument
against men"!   It is the one thing
Nature has not done.   Civilisation has, I
hope, accomplished this for us, but Nature
most distinctly has nothing whatever
to do with it.   The writer has apparently

forgotten that there was a time when
human beings were in a more "natural"
state than they can be said to be in now,
when the male's only form of courtship
was a struggle with the lady who had
engaged his affections, and that the female
always successfully resisted a suitor when
she had bestowed her preference on a
favoured rival. The confusion between
what is unnatural and what is unusual,
against which John Stuart Mill warned
controversialists on this subject, is again
apparent. "In the feudal ages," says
Mill, "war and politics were not thought
unnatural to women because not unusual."
How, even now, would "Nature" prevent
women at this moment from facing an
enemy, from donning a uniform, from
marching to the battle-ground? Let us
imagine all the available inhabitants of
Great Britain drawn up in battle array
opposite each other · men on one side
and women on the other. Given to
women a few generations of training such
as soldiers have had in discipline and
gunnery and all the paraphernalia of war,

34

given the same means of acquiring arms,
given the generalship of a Jeanne d'Arc,
given the numerical preponderance of
able-bodied women (a fact that I never
shirk, seeing that "Nature" provides the
world with a still greater preponderance
of male infants), given all these circumstances, I am not at all sure that "Nature"
would guarantee all the men invulnera-
bility from the female bullets.   It is true
that in sporting parlance the betting
would be perhaps 2 to 1 *on* the "favourite,"
which, in virtue of its greater familiarity
with the battlefield, would probably be
the male army.   But certainly Nature
would have nothing to do with prevent-
ing such a contingency in the unlikely
event of women making up their minds
to provoke the arbitration of war to
decide their claims.   But *because* the
possibility is that, should such a conflict
arise, men would probably be successful ;
is that really to be considered a sound
reason for denying the vote to women,
if it can be proved that it is demanded
by the majority of those willing to ex-

press an opinion on the subject ? In thus reducing the physical force argument to its final absurdity, let it be borne in mind that the statement that "force is the weapon that man alone can wield" is simply a mis-statement of facts, and very easily disproved. Force is not *only* exercised in antagonism ; we put forth force in every minute of our lives that we are not either asleep or ill. When we move or work we are exercising force, and when we read it is by latent force that we assimilate what we are reading. To talk of women as having been "deprived by Nature" of all "force" shows incredible looseness of thought, and to base an argument on so shallow and obvious a fallacy is an indication of the feebleness of a cause and the mental calibre of its supporters.

Assuming for a moment, however, that "physical force" should be given the limited application, which an exact or trained thinker would never apply to it, but which passes current for thought amongst the enemies of this movement, even so it does not carry the conviction

intended by those who use it to the minds
of any one who is capable of thinking for
himself. The following remark was delivered to a Cambridge audience by an
influential gentleman who presided at the
meeting, and who overlooked the initial
error of assuming that "force" was only
put forth during a struggle.

"Lastly, there is the physical force
argument; namely, that the ultimate
direction of affairs must be vested in those
who in their own persons possess the
fighting strength of the nation. This
argument goes far. In fact, it goes much
too far, and it proves that the vast majority
of Governments, that have ever existed,
were impossible. It proves that the
Government of Louis the Great of France
was impossible, because in his own person
he was unable to coerce the French nation.
It proves that any despotism is impossible,
and that any oligarchy is impossible. And
when I contemplate these results of the
argument, I wish it were true. But unfortunately it is manifestly false."

It is true, however, that I have found

myself in conversation with men who
have imagined themselves opposed to the
extension of the Parliamentary franchise
to women, and that, when I have suggested to these gentlemen that perhaps
their opposition was due to the fact that
women were not soldiers, they have indig-
nantly repudiated the idea that this fact
should influence their opinion, and have
contemptuously brushed it aside with an
impatient exclamation, saying, " No, no,
that is no argument." Yet it has been
and is used again and again by statesmen
and lawyers, such as Lord James and Mr.
Asquith, it was paraded again in a leading
article in the *Times* as lately as the 29th
Feb. last, and supported by correspondents
to the editor of the same newspaper, as
not only the strongest but the one unanswerable argument ; and it has been solemnly
advanced as the one conclusive argument
by a leading weekly journal, whose
standing in the intellectual world is
generally acknowledged. Were none of
its readers found willing to protest against
the inaccuracies and perversions perpe-

trated by the writer of the article under discussion ? it will be justly asked. The answer is, that in the only letter that appeared in reply, words occurred, in effect admitting the depressing " fact" that women do not possess physical force. And underneath this lady's letter was a note saying that hers had been chosen out of a great number that had reached the editor, and that there would be no further correspondence admitted on the subject.

I do not blame the lady who, although battling valiantly with her able foe, allowed the dust of rhetoric to blind her into unthinkingly accepting statements which contain glaring falsities, plainly apparent to those not thus blinded. It is, of course, difficult not to be dazzled by the illuminating rays that fall from a journal of the light, leading, and learning of the *Spectator*, but I have endeavoured not to allow my vision to be obscured by its intellectual magnificence in my efforts gently to question its soundness on a subject to which I have given many years of deep attention.

III

OBJECTIONS TO WOMEN'S SUFFRAGE CONSIDERED

THERE are two difficulties which beset those actively engaged on the work of this great movement. First, the existence of women to whom through ignorance or indolence the subject of their own enfranchisement does not appeal. Secondly, the inherent prejudices of some men. How are we to arouse the interest of the lethargic women, and to convince these men that it is no longer a subject for ridicule, and its supporters objects of scorn or aversion to their superior male tastes? Not by defiant self-glorification on the part of women, on the one hand, nor by fierce denunciation of men on the other; but by appealing to the instincts possessed by women in common with men—the desire for freedom, the demand for justice, and the hope of happiness. If our op-

ponents can be made to see that these
three great elements in national life are at
stake, our cause is won. For there are
few, if any, who would maintain even to
themselves that freedom, justice, and
happiness are the lawful heritage of the
male alone. If, however, a great and increasing number of women do feel that
their chances of realising these ideals are
impaired by their exclusion from the
parliamentary franchise, then those who
still desire, and have the power, to with-
hold this gift must give very convincing
and satisfactory reasons for their unwill-
ingness to grant what would appear to be
so obvious and reasonable a demand.

The purpose of this present chapter will
therefore be to examine as exhaustively as
possible all the objections that a pains-
taking inquiry has enabled me to collect
on this subject. These have been gathered
partly from the speeches and writings of
opponents speaking and writing deliberately on the subject, and also from the
opinions I have heard expressed in conversation by persons whose opinions would

carry weight. And from the latter I have never, even at the risk of wearying them, lost an opportunity of demanding and obtaining an opinion. Briefly summarised, the objections invariably take one or other of the following forms :—

1. That as women cannot, or do not, bear arms in defence of their country, therefore they should have no voice in its government. The next chapter is devoted wholly to the consideration of this objection.

2. That on physiological grounds they are unfit to vote.

3. That the home is the sphere of women.

4. That they are mentally and morally, as well as physically, inferior to men.

5. That they are represented by their male relations in the polling booth in whatever class of life they happen to be.

6. That women would be under the dominion of their ministers of religion.

7. That they have the first claims socially, and therefore do not need a vote.

8. That they suffer from no disability from the existing laws.[1]

9. That they would lose more than they would gain by having a vote.

10. That with the establishment of manhood and womanhood suffrage, which, it is argued, will be the inevitable outcome of the removal of the sex disability, there will be a numerical preponderance of women in the electorate.

11. And that this preponderance will work mischievous results to the nation owing to the emotional character of women.

12. Lastly, that women themselves do not want the vote.

The most formidable and the most plausible is the last-mentioned objection. It is probably true that those who advance this argument against Women's Suffrage are acquainted chiefly with women who are indifferent to the success or failure of this movement ; yet they cannot ignore the fact that during the last year the move-

---

[1] This contention is refuted in the essay that constitutes the last chapter in this book

ment has made enormous strides. Let justice be done to those women who for good or for ill have at least advertised their cause. Let it be recognised that at the present moment not only the "Press" in the United Kingdom but the "Press" in all civilised countries have been awakened to the fact that a serious suffrage agitation is on foot, and let the fact be acknowledged that the latest petition in favour of Woman Suffrage received 257,000 signatures. It is noteworthy that although since the year 1866 numerous petitions have been presented by women to Parliament demanding enfranchisement, and that during the period between 1870 and 1880 petitions were presented to the Commons with upwards of 2,000,000 signatures, there are only two protests on record. One of these nestled in the pages of the *Nineteenth Century*, in June 1889, and was supported by the signatures of 104 ladies. Its appearance promptly called forth a declaration in favour of Women's Suffrage the next month in the *Fortnightly Review*, to which the signatures of 2000 ladies were appended. A "petition" against Women's Suffrage has since been presented to Parliament bearing some hundred signatures, but the methods by which these signatures were obtained do not bear inspection and are of very doubtful value, as an expression of well-considered opinion. Against thousands ready to declare themselves in favour, no more than a few hundreds have ever been known publicly to declare themselves unfavourable; but until women's political organisations refuse to support any Government that does not officially adopt some measure to ensure the enfranchisement of women, so long will men be justified, or at least will justify themselves, in saying that women do not want the vote. But let it be conceded that except in so far as they are capable of recognising their common sisterhood, the vote will not affect individual women any more than it affects individual men, nursed in the lap of luxury—women whose connection with their less fortunate kind is limited to the opening of bazaars with a charitable purpose, or attending cere-

monies for the purpose of pronouncing
new hospitals open, or any other form of
dilettante philanthropy. But to those who
are inspired by the grand faith in universal brotherhood, whatever may be their
worldly position, the need appears as
urgent and imperative as to any of their
humbler sisters.

I would remind my readers that the
system of slavery in even its naked
brutality received support from some of
its victims. But the fact that there were
slaves who bitterly lamented their recent
bondage, does not make slavery less
abhorrent and the cause of freedom less
righteous. It is the educational value of
the vote that is its most important aspect ;
its wholesome stimulus to self-dependence
and self-respect, which shall evoke an-
swering qualities in the minds of men, and
so ensure the united progress of both sexes,
along the only paths by which it can possibly profit our common humanity to travel.

2. Then there are those who object
"on physiological grounds." By this we
suppose they refer to the supreme fact of

motherhood, actual and potential. But do they mean that because on women falls the chief responsibility, the whole of pain, and where there is any, all the disgrace of reproducing their species, they are therefore unfit for citizenship ? Even if this curiously paradoxical conclusion were an equitable one, we would remind those who arrive at it that although all mothers are women, all women are not mothers. And again, that even all the women who become mothers are not always either bearing or rearing children. There is often a period in early womanhood, and invariably in middle and old age, where those who do perform this duty to the State are entirely free from the direct responsibility attached to motherhood. Therefore, even if this function were a debarring incident, it would leave unaccounted for the prohibition suffered by the women who are not temporarily engaged in bearing children, and those who have ceased to rear or bear them. But it is hardly possible to conceive that any intelligent person seriously believes that the physical functions of women justly debar them from parliamentary representation, and were it not that I have found this very argument seriously advanced by what I had supposed to be a cultivated mind, I would not have troubled my readers with its refutation.

3. With those, on the other hand, who protest that the " Home is the sphere of women," I am thoroughly and heartily in accord. But those who would limit the interests of the home to food, and raiment, and furniture, travesty the worthiest development of civilisation. Mr. Fawcett said in the House of Commons :—

" I believe whenever you enfranchise a class, the first result of that enfranchisement is to make those who are enfranchised take a keener and a deeper interest in all that concerns the public affairs of the country. It does not draw them from their homes ; it does not draw them from their shops, it does not draw them from their daily labour ; but I believe that all experience will show that those who are the best workmen, those who are the best traders, and those who are the best merchants, are those who are the best citizens ; I believe that this will hold equally true when that day shall arrive when women who are ratepayers shall be enfranchised."

And is there one of us who has not gathered from his or her experience the fact that the mothers who are most useful in their homes, and most respected by their husbands and children, are those who are most keenly interested in all the concerns, not only of their immediate home, but of the universal asylum of the working world ? And those who have definite interests and occupations of their own are not only more interesting companions, but worthier guides to the aspirations of the generation dependent on them. If this can be conceded—and no one not disposed to controvert any and every opinion expressed by those they happen to disagree with will wish to dispute it—not only is it unnecessary to debar such women from voting, but those who do so are guilty of a waste of force almost incredibly stupid, in not making direct public use of that vastly beneficial element now used only spasmodically and indirectly in the government of their country.

4. Now those who object to conceding the vote to women on the ground that they are generally " inferior " to men, have never made it quite clear whether they mean that the last man is superior to the first woman. To those whose words are to be thus interpreted I have no answer. But of those who merely modestly assume that in each class and sphere the relative qualities of the female do not compare favourably with the corresponding qualities possessed by the male, I would ask, assuming this contention to be correct, does this failure of the aggregate female value to meet the total attained by the male value justify the representatives of the latter in excluding all the representatives of the former from participation in the privileges shared by even the illiterate among the more favoured sex ?

5. That women are represented by their male relations is an assertion made by men alone, and is contradicted by all their other

objections to extending the suffrage to women. Tennyson aptly says : " Woman is not undeveloped man, nor yet man's counterpart." Mrs. Browning also pointed out that " Womanliness was a positive thing not the negative of manliness."

6. Then we come to the cry that most women would be influenced by their priests or their doctors, or both. But Mr. S. Smith, speaking in the House of Commons, says that some of the leaders of the Woman Suffrage movement take strong objection to the existing marriage laws, and the relation of the sexes upheld by all branches of the Church, and he then asks, " Could a greater calamity befall the human race than to undermine this sacred institution ? " Yet another opponent, the American Bishop of Albany, in an article against Woman Suffrage, says : " There are two factors of grave danger in the political issues. First of all the religious question. . . ." He then goes on to say, " It is to the infinite honour of women that they are more quickly interested, more keenly concerned, and more deeply influenced in their religious feelings and convictions, than men."

THE HUMAN WOMAN

Is it possible to conceive of any quality the possession of which is to the *infinite honour of women*, being a mischievous and "dangerous" factor in political contests ? Thus we find that there are timid persons who see danger to their cherished institutions from the same source whence others fear that these very institutions will derive undue power.

7. How can any one honestly assert that women receive just social as against legal acknowledgment of their claims in view of the recent proceedings at Cambridge ? There, it will be remembered, women's simple, just, and, one would have thought, unanswerable claim to equal recognition for equal achievement in the matter of degrees, was treated in a manner reflecting lasting discredit on that noble seat of learning.

8. Many trivial advantages for which men sacrifice nothing, and which women could perfectly well do without, and which they would take their chance of retaining, women of a certain class certainly enjoy. But the laws of inheritance, also the laws relating to the maintenance of children, are flagrantly unjust to women, and in the divorce courts, in the labour markets, every-

where where it is possible, men cling to
their ill-gotten advantages, very often unconsciously even, with a tenacity which
nothing but equal recognition in the eyes
of the State will ever loosen.[1]

9. We have been warned that we will
lose more than we gain. Well, we are
willing to take the risk ! Experience does
not show that with increased privileges
comes less respect. Queen Victoria com-
manded no less respect in that she filled
an office usually the prerogative of men.
Neither would men respect women less if
they had a voice in the governing power
of their country. And notwithstanding
anything men may say to the contrary,
they know this to be a fact.

10. To some men the eventual possible
preponderance of women in the electorate
is a bogey (usually derided as petticoat
government) of so demoralising a nature
as to make this terrifying contingency
of itself outweigh any mere question of
justice. This objection should, however,
have no terror for the male voter, and

[1] See chapter on "Present Disabilities of the Woman of
England."

53

can have no logical standing whatever
except in the unlikely event of all women
being arrayed on one side of a question
and all men on the other. Should this
practically impossible eventuality occur,
and there happened at the time to be a
preponderance of women voters, I can
conceive no possible reason why they
should not reap the benefit of their unanimous majority. Nothing could prove
more conclusively the essential righteousness of the possession by women of the
vote ! But let it at least be remembered
that nature would not be responsible for this
result, as more male than female children
are born yearly in this country ; and at
the age of twenty males and females are
equal in number. But why the likeli-
hood of this strange unanimity of opinion
should be dreaded in women when such
a phenomenon has never been known
amongst men it is difficult to perceive,
except that the most extravagant, far-
fetched hypotheses are sometimes advanced
in defence of utterly illogical positions, and
desperately adopted in default of any sound
ground for attempting to defend the inde-

fensible. This improbable contingency, however, may fairly be said to represent the habitual political condition in which women move and have their being. On any question requiring legislation that affects women exclusively, if any legislation can be said to do so, women are not only outnumbered but non-existent. There is this difference between the two cases that women have not now, as these aggrieved and down-trodden men would have had in the hypothetical circumstance we are considering, the equal chance of fair representation. However, the immediate inclusion of women with the same qualifications that now give men the vote which is all the responsible societies ask for, would add less than one third more to the existing electorate. If, as is so often asserted, the demand for the vote is the cry of a very small minority amongst women, the number would not hastily be added to. If with its educative qualities the vote already possessed by women caused an increasing number to demand their inclusion it would at least prove that women suffered from their exclusion. By the time this dreaded "numerical preponderance" became a fact, if it ever should, which I doubt, the interests of men and women would be so merged that there never could arise a question on which all men and all women would be marshalled on opposite sides.

11. And, lastly, those must be dealt with who fear that the emotional instincts of women will have a mischievous effect upon the legislation of a country where female suffrage is an established fact. Mr. Asquith, in the House of Commons, said : "It is not for us to prove that the measure would work ill ; it is for the supporters of the measure to prove that it would work some good." We can only " prove " this by seeking an expression of opinion from competent authorities in a country where women do vote. And we find the House of Representatives in Wyoming passing the following resolution :—

"'That the possession and exercise of suffrage by the women in Wyoming for the past quarter of a century has wrought no harm, and has done great good in many ways ; that it has largely aided in banishing crime, pauperism, and vice from this

State, and that without any violent or oppressive legislation ; that it has secured peaceful and orderly elections, good government, and a remarkable degree of civilisation and public order ; and we point with pride to the facts that, after nearly twenty-five years of women suffrage, not one county in Wyoming has a poor-house, that our jails are almost empty, and crime, except that committed by strangers in the State, is almost unknown ; and, as a result of experience, we urge every civilised community to enfranchise its women without delay."

Here we would have thought that Mr. Asquith has what he asked for, but later on we find him saying, " It will be sufficient to point out that it is impossible to argue seriously from the experience of a rudimentary community like Wyoming, with a sparse population and . . . to the case of an ancient, complex, highly-organised society such as our own." It is easy enough to " point out " the " impossibility " of arguing seriously from the only direct evidence it is possible to produce in refutation of their evil prognostications,

but not so easy to convince thoughtful
people of the sincerity and "seriousness"
of an opposition which refuses to accept
the very test for which they clamour.
To them the opinion of competent persons
in New Zealand, Australia, and Idaho,
will be of little value. But all these
countries have, through their representatives, expressed themselves favourable
to the results which they ascribe to the
establishment of Woman Suffrage, and declare that they consider the results not
merely negatively harmless, but positively
good [1]

But we are entitled to ask, supposing
these opinions were adverse instead of
favourable, would our opponents feel the
same difficulty in judging from the results
in countries where the conditions are not
similar to our own ?

And in our own "highly civilised
country," whither are these emotional
tendencies supposed to lead us ? Surely
not in the direction of an ill-considered
war. The women of the twentieth

[1] See various expressions of opinion collected by the
Suffrage Societies on this subject.

century will not desire hastily to send their husbands and sons on expeditions involving risk to life and health. And in these days of competition, those women who have no husbands or sons will not rashly advocate schemes likely to diminish the supply of these commodities ; and should they be so forgetful of their interests, will there be no men left to instruct them and warn them of the abyss into which they are plunging ? If not into war then, into what other dangers is it feared the emotions of women would lead their unfortunate country, if they had their just share in directing its policy ? To such questions as these we never have had, and never are likely to have, any definite, reasonable answers. All the objections are based on vague and speculative generalities. And with those whose traditional policy it has been always to uphold and cling to privilege, I have no quarrel. Their attitude at least is intelligible. But the same cannot be said of those whose boast it is to preach freedom to the world, and whose watch-word is equality of opportunity for all human beings ; those who advocate the extension of the franchise to men in the spirit with which Mr. Gladstone uttered the following noble sentiments : " Give to these persons new interests in the Constitution, new interests *which by the beneficent processes of the law of Nature and of Providence shall beget in them new attachments ;* for the attachment of the people to the Throne, the institutions, and the laws under which they live, is, after all, more than your gold and your silver, more than your fleets or your armies, at once the strength, the glory, and safety of the land." Is there any one prepared to say that the beneficent processes of the law of Nature and of Providence works in and for men only ? Yet some of the very people who applaud these sentiments practically ignore the fact that if it be true of men it is true of women also. Some of our opponents feel the great democratic spirit urging them from within to an unwilling recognition of the justice of our claim, but they fence with their consciences, aided by the demon of sophistry, until it gives them temporary peace. It must have been in

some such mood that Mr. Asquith (who,
in his dealings with women's claims on
the London Government Bill, was recently
likened to the man in the parable who
said, " I go not," but went) gave utterance
to this curious contention, in speaking in
the House of Commons against the extension of the franchise to women : "*The
doctrine of democracy demands that we should
equalise where inequality exists among things
fundamentally alike, but not that we should
identify where things are fundamentally unlike.*" Now the hardest task Mr. Asquith
ever set himself, was to try and prove the
fundamental unlikeness of men and women
for political purposes. He talks of the
" inalienable difference of faculty and
function," for which " Nature herself "
is responsible. After all, let it be remembered that women enter life through
the self-same portals as do men, and the
choice of sex for self and progeny is, so
far, beyond human control ! From what,
then, does this inalienable difference of
faculty and function exempt women with
relation to the State ? Women, as well
as men, help to fill the State coffers ;

women, as well as men, contribute to the
local rates ; women, as well as men, pay
the penalty if they infringe the laws ;
women, as well as men, educate the young
of both sexes ; women, as well as men,
do work ; a larger proportion of one kind
of work falls to women, and a larger proportion of another kind falls to men.
Each contribute in their several capacities
to the well-being of their country. Unless
women's fundamental unlikeness to men
in these matters can be proved, Mr.
Asquith himself says that the doctrine
of democracy *demands* their enfranchisement ; for, in a quasi-democratic country,
such as ours, no one attempts to deny that
political freedom and justice are unattain-
able without representation.

Without true freedom, and without
real justice, happiness must necessarily be
of a limited kind. And yet the hope of
happiness is as sure a heritage of the
human female as of the male. Happiness
cannot be realised in its full perfection by
the masculine half of the globe's population, unless shared with and by the
feminine half Until the woman is given

full liberty to respond with her whole being—without any artificial restrictions as to her capabilities and functions—to the efforts initiated, if you will, by man in the direction of the perfection of the human race, the progress of the universal cause of truth· will be slow, spasmodic, and uncertain.

If it had been possible to put aside all prejudice and judge the question of whether or not women are entitled to enfranchisement fairly, and on its merits, Woman Suffrage would before now have been an established fact in England. But, unfortunately, the prejudice is so deep-seated, so inalienable from the deepest convictions of some men, and, with sorrow I admit it, of some women, that it has come to be regarded not as prejudice at all, but as the divine light of reason. This causes our opponents to adhere to their objections with a tenacity and fervour worthy of a better cause. Unfortunately, however, it is an attitude of mind which more often characterises the least worthy of fanatical beliefs. But we do not despair. Far from it! We believe

the day of Women's Freedom is at hand ;
when by the word " Nation " patriots of
both sexes will be recognised ; when the
inspiriting words spoken by the great
Liberal prophet in advocating the extension of the franchise to his fellow country-
men will apply with equal truth and equal
force to the women of his country :

" You will, as much as any former
Parliament that has conferred great legislative benefits on the nation, have your
reward,

'And read your history in a nation's eyes,'   .

for you will have deserved it by the benefits you will have conferred. You will
have made this strong nation stronger
still ; stronger by its closer union ; stronger
against its foes without, if and when it has
any foes ; stronger within by union between class and class, and by arraying *all
classes and all portions* of the community in
one solid and compacted mass round the
ancient throne which it has loved so well,
and round a constitution now to be more
than ever powerful, because more than
ever free."

64

IV

WAR AND THE WOMAN'S VOTE

THE moment seems opportune for prob-
ing the soundness of the oft-repeated
objection to conceding the just demand
of the tax- and rate-paying women of
Great Britain for Parliamentary representation, urged on the ground that as
women cannot or do not bear arms in
defence of their country they should
therefore have no voice in its government.

The grievance of the wealthy landlady
whose gardeners and grooms have votes
while she has none has been met by
asserting that she is merely one of a class
whose interests are represented by all the
male landowners. So be it. Let us agree
that legislation affecting the landed interest will be moulded by the votes of
her fellow-landowners. But war affects
all classes, and each unit in every class ;
and among the civilian population women
are affected by war at least as much as

are men.   If, then, for no other reason
than that their voice should be heard in
times when wars or rumours of wars are
rife, women should have votes.   Women
took as keen and intelligent an interest
in the progress of the last war in which
the nation engaged as their male relations;
and in such times any women worthy of
the name who, but for their sex, would
be entitled to vote, feel the injustice of
their exclusion from participation in the
election of their country's counsellors
as deeply and passionately as men would
feel a similar injustice.   As, however,
their alleged incapacity for military service has been insisted upon as a just
reason for so excluding them by legal
luminaries of such unquestioned intellectual attainments as Lord James of
Hereford and Mr. Asquith, and, as will
have been seen in the second Chapter,
as lately as February this year by a writer
in the *Spectator*, it is worth while further
to examine the depth and soundness of
this contention.

Now, can man's claim that he alone

is likely to possess sound judgment in the choice of counsellors be maintained upon the ground that it is he alone who is called upon to take up arms when the disputes of nations can be settled by no other means than brute force? It is argued that because woman is peaceful and has neither the inclination nor, possibly, the power to fight, it is a final reason for excluding her from any share in the council of nations—where, it might be supposed, brute force is not a factor.

But if the claim to enfranchisement is to be based entirely upon primitive instincts, then the instincts of women should be taken into account. The great maternal instinct which gives all mothers the power effectually to defend their young should be reckoned with. But war no longer depends upon the sudden ebullition of primitive instincts; it is a highly scientific game, and the actual combatants no more than pawns in the hands of those who move primarily in the matter. It is as absurd to say that a woman who contributes to the main-

tenance of the army and the State should
have no voice in choosing those whom
she thinks most likely to move wisely
and well in the matter, because she is
never likely to be called upon to fight,
as to say that no woman should order
any dish in her own house that she is
not herself prepared to cook ! Mr. Gladstone said, when advocating the extension
of the franchise to a class of men, not
then enfranchised, that the addition of
power to the State which would thereby
be assured was "more than your fleets
and your armies, at once the strength,
the glory, and the safety of our land."

A further illustration of the fatuity of
basing an objection to women's direct
participation in politics on the fact that
they are not actively concerned in mili-
tarism is afforded by a pronouncement
of Mr. Balfour's. In speaking of the
inadvisability of refusing to reward a
successful general on the ground that,
although the methods by which he obtained his success were approved of, dis-
approval of the cause was felt, Mr. Balfour

expressed the following sentiments, which evoked " loud cheers " :

" An argument like that requires our soldiers to mix themselves up in questions of policy—to consider not merely whether they are to obey an order, but what that order is that they are required to obey; and though I think we live in a country so happily circumstanced and with constitutional traditions so deeply based that we can hardly even conceive an interference on the part of the military power with the authority of the civilian power, yet, if such a thing were possible, the course I am commenting on would be the very course to bring it about, for a country in which the army concerns itself seriously with the question of policy is a country on the verge of a military despotism."

Now, I am not contending that because soldiers are not allowed to interfere in politics therefore women should have votes, but that if soldiers, as such, are not required to concern themselves with politics—or, in other words, with the

69

motives that govern their actions as soldiers—because they *do* fight, why are women to be debarred from directly concerning themselves in politics—or, in other words, in matters which affect them, as civilians, as much as they do men—because they do *not* fight ?

It is advisable, therefore, to see by what arguments those who put forward the objection support their position.

The objection that women are not competent to vote because no women are soldiers is generally founded not so much on the fact that they do not go on active service against a foreign enemy as on the other fact that they do not form part of that coercive force which is, in the last resort, at the back of all government. One policeman keeps five hundred people in order ; but that is because there are other unseen policemen, and ultimately soldiers, to be drawn on at need. Woman stands apart from all this, it is argued, and therefore government is not part of her business. Now this is certainly a plausible way of presenting a fallacy. Let us admit

the premise that " coercive force is at the
back of all government." But let us at
the same time analyse this coercive force.
What are its component parts ? Surely
it is not solely muscular and physical.
The training of the brain plays an even
more important part than the training of
the muscles in the skilful performance of
obedience-compelling actions. The acts
that are controlled by the knowledge of
the existence of a superior force behind
the apparent one—insufficient in itself to
control the otherwise unrestrained exhibition of certain tendencies, such as those
called forth by any strongly excited semi-
civilised crowd—are insignificant compared with the acts that are controlled
by the weight of public opinion. This
public opinion woman helps to form.
And it is the evidence of the stultification
of this immensely valuable moral force
which causes my profound belief in the
absolute necessity, if any united social or
moral progress is to be made, of taking
the female mind into consideration when
dealing with the government of a country

where laws of vital and sometimes exclusive interest to the female portion of the population are continually being passed. It will not, I think, be disputed that women do in a very marked degree exercise that " coercive force " in its most magnetic form, that is, at the back of all government. No one acquainted with the discipline of a women's college or a large public girls' school will wish to assert that the " coercive force " exercised by the head-mistress is not identical with that exercised by a head-master or a commanding officer. I have myself seen a hushed awe, almost amounting to an esoteric panic, overtake a large body of girls when the late Miss Benson, sister of the Archbishop, used to come suddenly upon them in the large day school at Oxford of which she was head-mistress. And this wholesome respect for authority, exemplified daily by the contact of any superior mind, or any representative of superiority with a mass of dependants, is not the result of physical fear, which the argument I have quoted would suggest,

72

nor are its influences either subjectively or objectively confined to one sex.

On April 29, 1892, the *Times*, in a leading article on Women's Suffrage, put forth the same idea in other words : " Men can demand a share of political power *which they are not particularly well fitted to use*,[1] because they possess *de facto* a share of the physical force upon which all political arrangements ultimately repose. Women do not possess such physical force, and, therefore, can prefer no such claim ! " Now the curiously loose way of thinking that seems to be considered good enough, passes current for serious reflection when used by men on this subject. The absurdity of men arrogating to themselves a monopoly of the physical force exercised by the human race does not seem to strike the people for whose benefit these arguments are advanced. Statements such as " Women do not possess such physical force," pass unchallenged. Why, Heaven only knows. Women do not, it is true, form part of the army or navy or police

---

[1] The italics are the writer's, not the quoter's.

force, with the exception in the last-named of female gaolers and female detectives ; but these professions do not exhaust or embody the whole physical force of the universe. Are all women born into the world devoid of muscles or of any muscular strength whatever ? Are they all cripples having no use for their limbs ? Is it forgotten that every civilised man is brought into the world in a healthy condition by protracted and agonising labour on the part of the woman, his mother ? Then let it also be remembered that in spite of the " indelible difference of faculty and function," for which "nature herself" is responsible, which Mr. Asquith[1] relied on to justify his opposition to female suffrage, women enter life through the selfsame portals as do men, and that the choice of sex for self and progeny is, so far, beyond human control ! Sydney Smith, in his work on " Female Education," sees no such " indelible difference." "For," says he, " as long as boys and girls run about in the dirt and trundle hoops

[1] Debate in the House of Commons, April 27, 1892.

together, they are both precisely alike. If you catch up one half of these creatures and train them to a particular set of actions and opinions, the other half to a perfectly opposite set, of course their understandings will differ as one or the other sort of occupation has called this or that talent into action. There is surely no occasion to go into any deeper or more abstruse reasoning in order to explain so very simple a phenomenon."

But almost from the cradle an artificial distinction between the sexes is created and fostered : self-reliance and self-control encouraged in the boy, and discountenanced in the girl. How often has a boy been told by his ignorant nurse, his ignorant governess, or his equally ignorant mother: "Don't cry—that is like a girl;" thus sowing the first seed for that contempt for women that some unfortunate men grow up with. And how many of us have had this irritating kind of experience ! Two children, a girl of ten and a boy of seven, who, with their governess, have just returned from a drive in their pony cart : the girl, to her delight, seeing no one in the stable-yard, eagerly begins to unharness the pony, when to her disgust the governess interposes with, " Let G——," three years the girl's junior, " do that ; that is not a girl's work." In further illustration of the obliquity of vision in regarding the relation of the sexes that is artificially stimulated by even the best-intentioned, I give an instance that occurred in a little journal purporting to be a guide to parents as to how to bring up their children on the most " enlightened " principles.

" My brother-in-law," says the writer of an article on " Punishments, their use and abuse," " was once in a hospital at Glasgow, when a little boy was incorrigible, and defied both nurses and doctors. At last a nurse fetched some little girl's clothes from a female ward and dressed him in these for a day, taking away his own. The effect was magical, and during the rest of his stay the sight of the girl's clothes was all that was needed to keep him in order."

This was *not* given as an instance of the possible abuse of punishment. It is on the contrary distinctly recommended, and is held up as an admirable and suitable punishment.

To my mind it is the most imbecile and impertinent (the word in both its true and its borrowed sense is applicable) punishment ever meted out to an obstreperous urchin.

"The effect was magical;" what does that mean? That the sense of degradation was so great that it produced a result which exhortation, example, kindness, and reason were powerless to effect. "If you *will* give so much trouble you shall be paraded as that degraded thing, a female child." If it was not meant to convey that idea to the child's mind, what was meant?

It could not be supposed to be the *unsuitableness* of the attire that produced this magical reform in the boy's conduct, otherwise the same punishment for a girl, *i.e.* to masquerade as a boy, would be considered beneficial. But dress a recalcitrant

77

girl in boy's clothing and she would delight in the freedom and the novelty ; she would not see anything in the punishment so terrible as to produce instant reformation.

This " punishment " laid in the boy a fertile seed, the inevitable fruit of which would be contempt for women. It was insistence upon sex at an age when there should be no sense of sex.

My baby of three (a boy) is sometimes dressed up in their games by his sisters and brother as a little girl ; but to him to personate a female child is a pleasure and a privilege. Was not his mother once a little girl ? Why associate her garb with humiliation and shame ?

The ignorant, smug, self-satisfaction with which this " brother-in-law's " example is advanced for our edification, without a qualm or doubt as to its perfect wisdom, is an illustration of the " enlightened " spirit in which our unfortunate boys are " educated." Then there are hypocritical and hysterical moanings over the way prostitution flourishes in this " civilised " country of ours.

WAR AND WOMAN'S VOTE

I do not know if the person who initiated this outrage was a doctor. If so, *cherchez la femme.* Probably in his case a triumphant rival woman medico. But it sounds more like a parson. That kind of "man of God" who ignores the divine charity and humility of his Teacher in insisting upon the brutal, or, as he would call it, "natural," dominance of the male, which there is not a word or hint in all Christ's teaching to support. It is true that Paul makes some uncalled-for remarks on the subject; but like the old Sabbatarian lady when reminded of the corn-plucking episode, "I think none the better of him for that."

"Was it," asks Dr. Emanuel Bonaria, in a treatise on "Women's Frontal Lobes," "Mary Somerville who had to hide her books and study mathematics by stealth after all the family had gone to sleep, for fear of being scolded and worried because she allowed her intellect full scope? She has now a bust in the Royal Institution ! Whatever view of the case theoretical considerations may suggest, there is one

79

fact beyond all cavil, and it is this : that the female frontal lobes are not only capable of equalling in power the male's frontal lobes, but can surpass them *when allowed free scope.* This has been recently proved in one of the Universities, where a woman[1] surpassed the Senior Wrangler in mathematics—an essentially intellectual work." This is not an isolated case. President White, of the University of Michigan, expresses himself thus : " For some years past a young woman has been the best scholar of the Greek language among 1300 students (male and female) ; the best student in mathematics in one of the classes of our Institution is a young woman, and many of the best scholars in natural and general science are also young women." Dr. Fairchild, President of the Oberlin College in Ohio, in which over 1000 students of both sexes study in mixed classes, says : " During an experience of eight years as Professor of Ancient Languages, Latin, Greek, and Hebrew, and in

---

[1] Miss Philippa Fawcett, University Examination, Cambridge, June 1890.

the branches of ethics and philosophy, and during an experience of eleven years in theoretical and applied mathematics, the only difference which I have observed between the sexes was in the manner of their rhetoric."

But this is a perhaps pardonable digression giving a few opinions of competent judges as to the mental capacity of women to compete and co-operate with men ; the immediate subject under discussion is their physical capacity in the same direction.

On this point we find Professors Geddes and J. A. Thomson, in their joint work on "The Evolution of Sex," expressing their opinion that "we need a new ethic of the sexes, and this is not merely, or even mainly, as an intellectual construction, but as a discipline of life, and we need more : we need an increasing education and civism of women." If we discard the ideal held forth in the nursery rhyme that the highest good that can be offered to women is

"To sit on a cushion and sew a fine seam,
And feed upon strawberries, sugar, and cream,"

81   F

we shall perhaps be led to sympathise with Mr. E. Wakeman, an American author, who, after visiting this country for the purpose of making observations, waxes enthusiastic over the " pit-brow lasses " of the Wigan district, and describes them as " strong, healthy, good-natured, and thoroughly respectable, altogether unlike the forlorn creatures bearing the image of woman " that he had expected to find them. " English roses glow from English cheeks," he continues ; " you cannot find plumper figures, prettier forms, and more shapely necks, or daintier feet, despite the ugly clogs, in all of dreamful Andalusia." He was astonished at the wonderful quickness of eye and movement shown by the " screeners," and by the superb physical development and agility of the " fillers." " Altogether," he concludes, " I should seriously regard the pit-brow lasses as the handsomest, healthiest, happiest, most respectable working women in England."

In less devitalised communities this magnificence of physique is, of course, less rare, and in the *Westminster Review*,

October 1865, the following testimony from a physician as to the prowess of certain African tribes is of interest : " I am a medical man. I have spent several years in Africa and have seen human nature among tribes whose habits are utterly unlike those of Europe. I had been accustomed to believe that the muscular system of women is necessarily feebler than that of men, and perhaps I might have dogmatised to that effect ; but to my astonishment I found the African women to be as strong as our men. Not only did I see the proof of it in their work and in the weights that they lifted, but on examining their arms I found them large and hard beyond all my previous experience. On the contrary, I found the men of these tribes to be weak, their muscles small and flabby. *Both facts are accounted for by the habits of the people.* The men are lazy in the extreme ; all the hard work is done by the women." And we read that "les femmes Sphakiates ne le cèdent en rien aux hommes pour la vigueur et l'énergie.

THE HUMAN WOMAN

J'ai vu un jour une femme ayant un
enfant dans les bras, et un sac de farine
sur la tête, gravir, malgré ce double
fardeau, la pente escarpée qui conduit
à Selia."[1] Thus showing that maternity
does not necessarily impair a woman's
strength. Nor are individual instances
wanting where women have shown themselves able to hold their own in physical
competition with the strongest of men.
The *Manchester Evening Mail* of August
15, 1892, reports the following case:
" An ailing ' navvy,' who has been engaged
in some works near Versailles, was a few
days ago admitted to a hospital in that
town. Before the sick person had long
been in the institution it was discovered
that the apparent ' navvy ' was a woman.
The superintendent of the hospital was
not in the least surprised on hearing of
the transformation scene, for it appears
he was accustomed to deal with many
women who enter the hospital in male
attire. It is common in the district (says
a Paris correspondent) for robust women

[1] Jules Ballot, *Histoire de l'Insurrection Crétoise*

to don men's garb in order to obtain remunerative employment as navvies, porters, farm labourers, road-menders, bricklayers, masons, and builders. It has long been established that the average Frenchwoman of town or country has as great a capacity for work either in counting-houses, shops, fields, or farms, as her lord and master has for laziness, lolling in the cafés. . . ."

In the same month in the same year the *St. Petersburg Journal* reported that "ces jours-ci sera érigé à Sébastopol le monument élevé à l'honneur des femmes de cette ville qui en 1854 ont construit seules une batterie contre les troupes alliées. C'est une pyramide taillée en granit d'une hauteur de cinquante pieds. Sur un côté est écrit en lettres d'or ' C'est ici que se trouvait la batterie des Femmes,' sur l'autre face les mots suivants sont gravés : 'A cet endroit en 1854 les Femmes de Sébastopol ont construit une batterie.' " And Jeanne d'Arc is not the only other instance where women have taken their share in the defence

of their country.   In April 1892 the
Vienna correspondent of the *Standard* reported that " on the 30th ult. there died
in Hungary at about the same hour two
ladies who served in 1848 in the Revolu-
tionary Army and fought in several of the
fiercest battles dressed in military uniform.
One of them was several times promoted,
and, under the name of Karl, attained the
rank of first lieutenant of Hussars.   At
this point, however, an artillery major
stopped her military career by marrying
her.   The other fought under the name
of Josef and was decorated for valour in
the field.   She married long after the
campaign.   An Hungarian paper referring
to the two cases says that about a dozen
women fought in 1848 in the insur-
rectionary ranks."   .

In the year 1900 women showed themselves eager to share the burdens of war
and even the dangers entailed.   In the
daily papers of May 11 of that year, it
was stated that President Kruger had
received a telegram from a female burgher
asking if the time has not yet arrived for

the formation of a corps of women, and stating that she was prepared with a body of women volunteers to take up arms in defence of their independence. This desperate offer of help may raise a smile, but at least these ladies were entitled to the sympathy not extended to the excitement-mongers of the butterfly order who, misrepresenting their sex and country, flitted aimlessly in the vicinity of the battlefield, earning the just condemnation of all those of both sexes responsible for the welfare of the sick and wounded. And it is actually recorded[1] how some o the Boer men refused to allow their wives to remain in their homes, as, owing to the fact that they were exceptionally good shots, their presence was considered indispensable in the laagers ; while the women who did remain completed by themselves the work of harvesting necessarily left undone by the men.

History therefore affords a complete refutation of the misconception as to the necessary inferiority in physical capacity

[1] Daily papers, March 3, 1900

of women to men, and when it is assumed
that men possess a monopoly of physical
strength and endurance the fact is overlooked, that many more soldiers die from
sickness and exhaustion than from wounds
received in battle. In the Franco-German
War there were four times as many ; in
the Russo-Turkish War the proportion
was sixteen to forty-four ; in the recent
Spanish War in Cuba the proportion was
still higher ; there were ten who died
from disease to one who fell in action.[1]
And in the daily papers of Wednesday,
June 27, 1900, we read that in the official
table of casualties in the South African
War, deaths from disease had then mounted
up to 3985, whereas the number who
had been killed in action or who had
died of wounds was no more than 2973.
Again, of 16,358 sent home as incapable
of service, more than 12,000 were returned
as sick, and less than 4000 as wounded.
M. Bloch says : " In two weeks' time after
the French army is mobilised it is the
expectation of the best authorities that

[1] *The Future of War*, by M. de Bloch.

they would have 100,000 men in hospital, even if never a shot had been fired." The percentage of sick and suffering in an army of women might possibly be higher still, but a certain amount of work would be got through and hardship endured, and shots fired, by those who had felt capable of enlisting, in spite of their sex. It is not, however, to advocate an army of Amazons that I am writing. Notwithstanding the opinion of Socrates, the "first martyr of intellectual liberty,"[1] in whose Ideal State "men and women are to have the same employment (for there is no real difference between the sexes)," says Socrates, "and they will go out to war together," may God forbid that there should ever be more than a few scattered examples of fighting women. But when an argument is based on a false assumption facts have to be focussed and brought into proportion before the value of such argument can be correctly estimated.

Another favourite way some people have of putting the same objection to

[1] Macaulay's "Essay on Bacon"

89

granting women the suffrage on the ground of their alleged incapacity for military service is : that as women are unable to perform the chief duty of citizenship they are not entitled to the privileges of citizenship. Now these persons base their argument on three assumptions : (1) that all women are necessarily incapable of military service ; (2) that the defence of their country against a foreign enemy is the chief duty of citizenship ; (3) that failure to fulfil this estimate of the duty of citizenship, notwithstanding the fulfilment of all the remaining duties and responsibilities of citizenship, is a just cause for debarment from participating in the *only* privilege of citizenship.

Now history has shown that, given the need and the opportunity, women are not incapable of serving their country as soldiers, and as leaders of an army. This disposes of the validity of the argument from a theoretical standpoint, and it would be extremely inadvisable to put it to a practical test ! Still, those who advance

this argument cannot have it both ways.
Either nature is responsible or custom.
The testimony of all historians and scientific explorers into the habits of savages
precludes the notion that the female under
natural, uncivilised conditions is inferior
to the male in strength, courage, or endurance. If then custom is responsible, it
does not necessarily follow that custom
is infallible, nor that a set of conditions
arising out of artificial circumstances are
necessarily too sacred to be disturbed, nor
that the usages established as a corollary
of these customs are final and inviolable.

Then as to the second assumption.
There were at the last census 29,002,525
adult inhabitants in Great Britain. Of
these 29 million odd adults, 171,000 go
to form the regular army; 491,000
civilians composing the volunteers and
yeomanry give a fraction of their time to
military service. In the same year in
which the census took place from which
the above figures are taken, the army of
the British Empire, including the reserves
and forces in India, numbered 616,642 of

those classed as effectives. The navy, including men and boys, 4200 coastguard, and 13,879 marines, and including also reserves, volunteers, and others, numbers 97,548. Then, after extracting 129,122 adult paupers, 58,196 adult lunatics, and the 12,541 adult inhabitants of H.M.'s prisons, there remain 28,052,000 persons. Thus about 2½ per cent., or only a little over 700,000 in every 29 millions of the adult population, are ever called upon actively to defend the empire against foreign enemies. The rest are employed in various other ways in contributing to the prosperity of their country. And in this category there is a numerical preponderance of several thousand women over men (for which nature at least is not responsible, there being actually more male infants born than female, as the devotees of " Nature " cannot be too often reminded[1]). Various causes contribute to this effect : the greater number of pursuits endangering life in which men are engaged, the preponderance of male over

[1] See p. 54.

female convicts, the greater proportion of male emigrants, and possibly the greater intelligence exercised by women in the care of their health.

One Member of Parliament who took an active part in the debate on Woman Suffrage, Mr. Radcliffe Cook, maintains that his opposition to Woman's Suffrage " rests on a different ground to that usually taken ; " and we are in this position · that any argument, worthless or otherwise, has to be faced. As John Stuart Mill said : " On every other subject under the sun but this one the burden of proof is supposed to lie with the affirmative," in this case with those who assert women's unfitness for enfranchisement. However, Mr. Radcliffe Cook's modest and scientific contribution to the argument against extending the franchise to women runs thus : " Everything that enables us to enjoy a high state of civilisation is due to the labours of men." " This" as Mrs. Fawcett observes, " would be a first-rate argument but for one fatal defect—it is obviously and absurdly untrue." In an account of

the Woman's Exhibition at Earl's Court
in the *Westminster Gazette* of the year
1904, May 4th, these words occur :
" Visitors will find themselves surrounded
by the work of women *and by countless
evidences of the beneficent influence of woman
on the world's progress.*" " Conceive," Mr.
Radcliffe Cook continues, " if it be possible, the sudden and simultaneous destruc-
tion of everything made by the hands of
men, and what would remain ! " What
a fruitless conception ! As fruitless as the
same conception would be substituting
the word " women " for " men " in the
above sentence. For " the business of a
woman's ordinary life," says Mill,[1] " is
things in general, and can as little cease to
go on as the world to go round."

If, however, it can be conceded that, in
every department of life for which they are
fitted, women fulfil their duties adequately
as responsible human beings, there is in
this fact no *prima facie* evidence that they
would not so fulfil the additional responsibility and duty involved by honourable

[1] " Subjection of Women."

parliamentary representation. Nor can it be estimated with any capability of proof, or demonstration of probability even, that all these manifold duties and responsibilities are insignificant contributions to the State compared with the service rendered by its soldiers and sailors. It is on account of the vastness and importance of this country's civil interests, to which women contribute their full share, that an army or navy is necessary at all. And it is putting the cart before the horse to ascribe greater importance to the one that is the outcome of the other.

Then, if the third assumption involved in this particular form of "objection" is valid, if incapacity for military service is indeed to be a debarring incident to legislative privileges, all the men who fail to pass the requisite medical examination would necessarily be disfranchised ; whereas as a matter of fact the incapacitated man returns to his civil duties, exercises his vote, while the man who is on active service, during an election necessarily loses his.

M. de Bloch, who has been hailed as the " greatest prophet of the age," goes so

far as to say that he believes that "war
will be decided not by these things—not
even by fighting men at all, but by factors
of which at present they take far too little
account. Primarily, the quality of tough-
ness or capacity of endurance, of patience
under privation, of stubbornness under
reverse and disappointment. That element in the civil population will be more
than anything else the deciding factor in
modern war. Then men at the front will
very speedily be brought to a dead-lock.
Then will come the question as to how
long the people at home will be able to
keep on providing the men at the front
with the necessaries of life. That is the
first factor. The second factor which
perhaps might take precedence of the
moral qualities is whether or not it is
physically possible for the population left
behind to supply the armies in front with
what they need to carry on the campaign."
The greater number of men fighting the
greater will be the proportion of the
women left, and the more anomalous their
position as unenfranchised householders
who have to suffer extra taxation and see

their money spent without the smallest choice on their part as to how it should be spent. The more military we become as a nation, the more need will the country have of the services of women in every other department of life. Women are gradually establishing themselves in the labour markets, they are creeping into the professions in spite of the most violent and unscrupulous opposition from some of the men who already occupied the field. I should like, however, at this point to express deep appreciation of the dignified protest recently made by certain male physicians, when the remuneration offered to medical women inspectors for doing precisely the same work that they had been appointed to do, was considerably less than they themselves received. These are signs of the times. The fact that these women should have been offered less is a disgrace ; that they compel respect in their own profession shows that women doctors and women surgeons are holding their own in the medical world.[1]

[1] The Women's Hospital at 144 Euston Road, London, is staffed, and managed, and maintained entirely by women, and a study of their latest report will repay perusal

97   G

THE HUMAN WOMAN

The distinguished army physician, Dr. Billroth, says that it would be necessary to have as many hospital attendants as there are soldiers in the fighting line if the sick and wounded are to receive adequate attention. Instances are not unknown of women surgeons performing operations on the battlefield with as much skill and coolness as are attributed to men. If, as has been justly said, taxation is not the only thing that justifies the demand for representation, then the work, the professional skill, and the initiative and executive capabilites of women should receive recognition and should be represented in the councils of the nation.

And from a practical point of view it is worth while to draw attention to the fact that during the South African War the colonies, New Zealand among them, where women suffrage is an established fact, were among the first to offer and to send troops in aid of the Mother Country.

The ultimate decision in this matter will not rest on even the aggregate opinion of men as to the desirability or otherwise of any change in woman's position relative to the State, nor on the computed gain or

loss in mental or physical ease that individuals may hope or fear, but on an estimate of the certain benefits which would
thereby accrue, first of all to the State,
secondly to women as a whole, and thirdly
to men, through the improvement in
women's mental and legal status. For
although the first obvious gain would be
to women, there would inevitably be a
corresponding gain for men and a conse-
quent gain—and this is by far the most
important aspect of the whole matter—to
the entire population.

"Whatever has been said or written
from the time of Herodotus to the present
of the ennobling influence of free government—the nerve and spring which it
gives to all the faculties, the larger and
higher objects which it presents to the
intellect and feelings, the more unselfish
public spirit, and calmer and broader
views of duty that it engenders, and the
generally loftier platform on which it
elevates the individual as a moral, spiritual,
and social being—is every particle as true
of women as of men."

Does the woman live in whose heart

these noble words of Mill do not find an echo ? Does the man exist who would persist in his conduct if he were persuaded that by withholding this freedom from women he is inflicting on them a wrong of which they are themselves only partially conscious ? Surely few men would from purely selfish motives continue to bar the entrance to this wider life, this more useful sphere, into which women would generally bring only that portion of themselves that was noblest, purest, and most spiritual.

The time has therefore come for men to examine their consciences, and say whether they will continue to take the responsibility of refusing what seems to those who have earned their right to be heard a simple claim for common justice.

NOTE —The two foregoing chapters were translated into French, and read as a paper at the *Congrès International de la Condition et des Droits des Femmes* in September 1900, in Paris The following note was appended by M Viviani, then Minister of War : "' Les femmes et le droit de guerre' Ce rapport est tout à fait remarquable. Le droit de la femme de voter est établi avec force. On ne peut le résumer. Il résume lui-même tous les arguments en faveur de la thèse. Rapport philosophique "

V

THE THREATENED RE-SUBJEC-
TION OF WOMEN

A REPLY TO LUCAS MALET

HAS Lucas Malet exhausted her powers of
imagination in her powerful, but perhaps
over-imaginative works of fiction that she
has none left for the destiny of the human
race ?   For while subscribing with humble
enthusiasm to her almost unrivalled achievements in the region of fiction, it is wholly
without trepidation that I venture to dispute her conclusions as to the origin, progress, present results, and future fate of
the Woman's Movement.

Lucas Malet quotes President Roosevelt's message wherein he says: "The
prime duty of man is to work, to be the
bread-winner ; the prime duty of the
woman is to be the mother, the housewife."
These utterances, she says, will appeal to
those of us who are neither *féministes* nor

wholly frivolous, "as sane and sound, a
return to the right reason and common-
sense."

Now, apart from the fact, which Lucas
Malet has either overlooked or is unconscious of, that 82 per cent. of the adult
female population have already been forced,
by the exigencies of modern life, into the
labour market, the view that the object for
which each man should work should be
merely to maintain his home, is on a par
with the view that women should exist
for no other purpose than child-bearing
and housewifery. What a terribly lack-
lustre ideal for both the man and the
woman ! The man is to work merely for
the sake of keeping body and soul together
on this earth. The woman is to bear
children and " keep " the home the man has
" worked " for. How cut and dried and
uniform and unspeakably dull it sounds !
But I do not wish to be misunderstood :
I claim that for women there is no greater
joy on earth, when it is a joy, than the joy
of motherhood. But if this and the cares
of the housewife were the only means of
self-expression open to a woman, I much

doubt if even her motherhood itself would constitute so great a joy. I brave the sniff that the phrase "self-expression" may excite. It has, I am aware, been used as a vehicle for much that is morbid and neurotic among the heroines of modern fiction. Nevertheless I use it advisedly. I mean that given the possession of the intensest joy a mother is capable of feeling in her relation towards her children, her husband, and her home, and given the fulfilment of her duties towards all three to the most conscientious heights attainable, it is not enough to occupy a fully-equipped, intellectual, healthy human female, any more than it would be enough for a fully-equipped, intellectual, healthy human father, whose delight in his children, his wife, and his home is often no less great than the mother's.

It is the recognition of this great and pregnant fact that, to my mind, constitutes the importance of the Woman's Movement. And it is just this awakening that, except in flashes and at rare intervals, Lucas Malet has failed in her article to take into account. If, then, the truth of this view can be conceded, wherein does the sanity and reasonableness lie that would prevent this *natural* if dormant desire of the human female to work and to *achieve* from finding expression? The desire to participate in the work of the world's progress, as well as to accept her mission to reproduce her species, is a natural desire.

In insisting, as I have done, on that grossly misused word *natural*, I range the whole force of biological research against those who see in women's subjection to men a "natural state of things." I recommend to those interested in this side of the question Professor Lester F. Ward's learned but engrossing work, "Pure Sociology": "A treatise on the organ and spontaneous development of Society," from which I may be permitted to make a few quotations. In the chapter on "The Phylogenetic Forces," after dealing exhaustively with what he calls the androcentric and gynœco-centric theories, he says: "The female is not only the primary and original sex, but continues throughout as the main trunk,

while to it a male element is afterwards
added for the purpose above explained.
The male is, therefore, as it were, a mere
after-thought of nature" (p. 314). He talks
of the proof of the gynœcocentric theory,
that is female rule, as " forced or wrested,
as it were, from unwilling minds by the
mass of evidence " (p. 316). " The female
not only typifies the race but, metaphor
aside, she *is* the race" (p. 323). "In a broad
general sense the relations of the sexes
throughout the animal kingdom might be
characterised as a gynœcocracy, or female
rule, but I propose to restrict the term, as
did Bachofen, to the human race and to a
phase of the early history of man which,
though almost unknown prior to the aston-
ishingly erudite and exhaustive researches
of Bachofen, is now known always to have
existed and still to exist at the proper status
of culture or stage of man's history " (p. 337).
Professor Ward recognises the fact that
this view is a great stumbling-block to
those who accept the existing state of
things as " divine " or " natural " in the
following passage : " *Women in History.—*

THE HUMAN WOMAN

" The series of influences which we have been describing had the effect to fasten upon the human mind the habit of thought which I call the androcentric world view, and this has persistently clung to the race until it forms to-day the substratum of all thought and action. So universal is this attitude that a presentation of the real and fundamental relation of the sexes is something new to those who are able to see it, and something preposterous to those who are not. The idea that the female is naturally and really the superior sex seems incredible, and only the most liberal and emancipated minds possessed of a large store of biological information, are capable of realising it " (p. 364).

Lucas Malet is obviously imbued with what Professor Ward calls the andro-centric world view, and seems sublimely unconscious that there is any other with an undisputed claim to respect. She thus, in her mind, and it appears sub-consciously all through her article, regards the supporters of Women's Emancipation Movement, as eccentric cranks or faddists, whereas they are, in truth, the normal reasoners Nowhere is Lucas Malet's "Androcracy" more amusingly evident than in the following passage : " His [man's] weaknesses—and even his warmest advocates cannot but own that you have but to see enough of him to know that he has many, and those by no means exclusively of the proverbially masculine type—are patent to her " [the Woman " who has tasted the sweets of independence "]. Is this meant humorously ? If so, the parenthesis makes the humour too subtle. This idea expressed in other words might run : " Man is not *really* perfect, you know ; we all think him so, of course, but he has his little flaws, as some of us with tremendous perspicacity are able to discover."

If the subjection of women can be shown to be a non-natural—which describes the condition better than unnatural —state, how is the fact of their subjection explained ? This is a perfectly legitimate query, and one which I shall attempt in as few words as possible to answer. It

was necessary and inevitable for the
purpose of developing the race. If the
female alone had continued to be *the
race*, and the male only the fertiliser, the
human race would never have emerged
from its embryonic state, and would have
remained in the same condition as the
animal tribe immediately below the
human tribe. The maternal instinct
existed ; and the human female, in common with all mammals, recognised and
cared for her own young. But the
instinct of fatherhood was a much later
development ; and simultaneously with
the taking on of the responsibility of
parenthood by the male did the female
lose her status as the supporter of the
family. The increased size of the male
was due to the female, through the law
of sexual selection. By degrees the male
discovered that it was less trouble to
capture the female at first than go through
the preliminary stage of fighting for her
with other males. So surely as the pre-
dominance of the female in the first
instance was overcome by the predomi-

nance of the male in the evolutionary process of race-building, so surely will the present gradual but unmistakable rise of the female continue for the benefit of the race until the right and true relations of the sexes are established, in such a manner as shall ensure the continued progress of the race along the lines of least resistance, and in the way best calculated to perfect it. To speak of the movement as a transitory wave already on the decline seems due to an extraordinary inability to grasp the goal towards which the human race is inevitably creeping. It seems almost incredible that a thinking being should consider that the minute period, in proportion to the ages, during which we have been able to register results, should be considered of sufficient length to enable us to form a judgment either of approval or condemnation of the effects of any given movement. The world's duration has been aptly compared to the hands of a clock in their twelve hours' journey round the dial ; eleven solemn hours having slowly struck and the minute hand having begun its last hour's round, not until about twenty minutes to twelve did the prehistoric period cease, at less than five minutes to twelve we entered upon our present state of comparative civilisation ; and the Women's Movement has been barely as a single tick of the second hand. What fools are rash enough to condemn a movement when the clock, having slowly struck twelve, the hands begin again their eternal journey : this one second counting but its own infinitesimal share in the march of eternity ?

The " artificial nomad " described by Lucas Malet may exist, and her life be drear and loveless, but what movement has not had its martyrs ? If incidentally the movement produces a few abnormal specimens it cannot be helped, but surely even they are better than the alternately smirking or fainting female she has superseded ? And I enter my protest most strongly against the view that the newest of the new women need necessarily be the " sexless, homeless, unmaternal " crea-true Lucas Malet paints. I maintain that it is possible to feel the *Zeit-geist* surging through one's inmost being, filling one with a desire to help forward in the right direction this supreme movement initiated by the "mysterious influence, coming one knows not whence, and sweeping over the minds of nations as the wind sweeps over a field of wheat," and yet be as truly and lovingly domestic as the most cosily old-fashioned could wish.

Whether we approve or not, the movement is here. The task nature has set herself through the subjection of women has been fulfilled ; women's unconscious mission, operating by natural laws, has hitherto been to humanise the male. By the law of interlocked heredity the race has now sufficiently advanced for women to have a conscious mission : the perfecting of the human race.

What should we think of the woman or of the man who would wish to re-establish gynœcocracy on this planet ; who would voluntarily aid and abet the reversion of the male to his original place in the economy of race-production as the

fertiliser, the fighter, and the hunter?
From the human standpoint we should
regard that man or that woman as an
enemy to progress and civilisation. And
yet there are thousands of men and women
in this identical position. By desiring to
maintain the subjection of women—a state
incidental to racial progress established in
order to raise the male to a position of
equality with the woman—these people
are in very deed enemies to their own
kind ; moles crawling in benighted regions
of their own making, unconscious of the
beautiful world above and around them.
They are the fools who whisper in their
hearts " there is no God."

Who has not noticed that it is always
the least virile and manly amongst the
men who are so bent upon " keeping
women in their proper place" (what
they really want, of course, is to keep
them out of it), and the least womanly
amongst the women who are willing
to abdicate their God-given right of
human will in favour of an unlovely
subservience to the mere brute strength

of the male.[1] This is what Lucas Malet observes when she sees the "highest class" least affected by " the new *régime*." The more intellectual and the better-bred the man, the less irksome in his domination to the woman. If it exists she does not feel it. It is for this reason that the supporters of this movement, with, as Lucas Malet observes, " one or two well-known exceptions," are not drawn from the aristocratic classes. But it is not to their credit. Because they suffer no visible or immediate inconvenience such as their less fortunate sisters daily experience, their interest, through lack of intelligence or intellectual sympathy, has not been quickened in the deep pulsating movement that is throbbing in the hearts and minds of all women—unconsciously in those who are affected by their disabilities, and consciously in those of the few who in all ages would have been the leaders in any movement they believe to be for the good of their kind.

Lucas Malet throughout her article

[1] See p. 219.

ignores the love of work for its own sake,
yet this love exists and is instinctive in
women as well as in men, and shows itself
very early in the child. The suppression
of one natural instinct cannot act beneficially upon another natural instinct, and
it is only when the human being has
been allowed to develop in the fullest
freedom that the true relations of the sex
function will assume its proper proportion.
Lucas Malet talks of the "American
climate making for the development of
nervous energy rather than that of sex."
It has, perhaps, never occurred to her
that the whole human race has become
artificially over-sexed, and that this condition, so far from being beneficial to the
race, is just one of those things that this
movement will tend to counteract. In
Mrs. Stetson's "Women and Economics"
this view is very ably and convincingly
demonstrated; I consider the book one
of the most illuminating treatises on the
whole of this question that has ever
been written.

Again I must insist that when speaking

of the over-sexed condition of the human race I utterly repudiate any participation in the belief that a sane, healthy desire for expansion and independence in the woman leads to the absurd views about child-bearing that Lucas Malet seems to think obtain amongst the mass of the would-be emancipated. But neither do I accept President Roosevelt's views as a doctrine of salvation. There is a great deal of loose talk about the necessity of large families for the good of a nation. Lucas Malet quotes President Roosevelt as follows : "If a race does not have plenty of children, or if these children do not grow up, or if when they grow up they are unhealthy in body, stunted or vicious in mind, then the race is decadent," &c. This does not strike me as very sound reasoning.

1. If a race does not have plenty of children it is decadent.

2. If it has " plenty of children," but they die, it is decadent.

3. If it has plenty of children and they grow up unhealthy and vicious, it is de-

cadent. But if a race managed to have fewer than " plenty," and they grew up healthy, well developed, and virtuous, would the race still be decadent without the " plenty " ? Is not the quality rather than the quantity of children the thing to be aimed at ? If, then, by improving women's status the breed improves, as improve it must, is not this preferable to the " plenty " in their present very mixed condition ? Has no one sufficient imagination to see in their mind's eye a race that would be incapable of breeding this mass of " undesirable aliens " who are tossed about from shore to shore, welcome nowhere, and a curse to themselves ?

We are in the transition stage ; and in this stage there always has been, always will be, disheartening phases. But let us not on that account talk of " going back " ; there is nothing, *nothing* that even the most conservative amongst us need wish to go back to. And if we set our ideal high enough and move steadily forward we may reach heaven at last.

116

VI

ON WOMEN IN ASSEMBLIES

SUPPORTERS of the Women's Suffrage
movement are often questioned as a final
test of their impracticability as to whether
or no they desire women, when they have
obtained the vote, to sit in Parliament.
Now, the official answer to that, from the
point of view of the Suffrage Societies,
is that they are all solidly unanimous in
asking for the extension of the franchise
to duly qualified women on the same
terms as it is, or may be granted to
men. As a united body we make no
further demand. That having been said,
and if the "danger" of women sitting
in Parliament is so grave a stumbling-
block to certain individuals who would
otherwise be willing to grant this elementary measure of justice, let them safe-
guard their position by curtailing the
extent of freedom conceded to women

within statutory limitations. The "thin end of the wedge" theory need not unduly alarm them, in view of the extreme difficulty electors, desirous of amending the statutes to the simplest extent, invariably encounter. Not until there was an urgent and insistent demand, and not until the indisputable advisability of removing this disability was apparent to a vast majority of the constituencies would there be any chance of its being removed, and then even the chance would not necessarily become a certainty.

For my own part, I always frankly avow, when I am asked the same question, that I see absolutely no objection to women serving their country as members of Parliament, if and when they should have been elected. It seems necessary to remind some people that the exercise of a vote does not necessarily entitle the voter to a seat in Parliament! If, however, a majority of the voters, male and female, in any given constituency, after a woman has gone through all that is involved in an electoral contest, deliberately choose

to elect their candidate, and she happens
to be a woman, the chances are she is
better fitted to serve than the majority
of men who are elected to the same
position. Now, I say *better* fitted advisedly
and out of no mere spirit of sex-laudation,
and for this reason, that already in municipal elections it has been shown that
more is expected in the way of competence
in a female candidate than in a male. At
the last annual meeting of the Women's
Local Government Society this particular
fact was commented upon by several
speakers: "The standard required for
a woman," said one of the first elected
women-councillors under the new Act,
"who is to be a candidate for a new
body, the time she is expected to give
to it, and the training she has had for
it, are enormously higher than that for a
man." And it is so. A man's qualifications for the public unpaid posts to which
he is aspiring are more or less taken for
granted, whereas a woman is required to
give some guarantee of fitness for what she
is undertaking. And it will be admitted

that she is generally able to do so. Whereas, in the words of Mr. Dyke Acland : "the average country guardian" described in his admirable paper on County Councils and Rural Education is one who "watches far more carefully over the rates than over any other subject entrusted to his charge." But among such men, of whom it cannot be said that this is the paramount consideration, there is a surprising unanimity of opinion as to the incalculable value of women's co-operation in their work.

Mr. Wyndham Holgate, Inspector of Workhouse Schools for Metropolitan District, says : " First to deal with Boards of Guardians. . . . There are many matters in which a woman's views and assistance are of great value in Poor-Law Work, but there is not time to go into them now. Should the present members of the society feel unequal or unwilling to come forward, I trust they will not rest satisfied until they have secured the election of a lady thoroughly supporting their views on every Board of Guardians in which they are interested."

WOMEN IN ASSEMBLIES

Lord John Russell, in an Opening Address at the Association for the Promotion of Social Science, Liverpool, spoke with prophetic solemnity as follows : " Every one must have observed the new influence which is falling to the lot of women in swaying the destinies of the world. . . . It seems to me that if the young generation are to be an improvement on their fathers, if sin is to have less dominion and religion more power, if vice is to be abashed and virtue to be honoured, it is to woman we must look for such a generation."

Lord Basing, formerly President of the Local Government Board, was of opinion " That there is a most useful function for women in connection with the administration of the Poor Law, and I hope as time goes on to see more women elected and serving as Guardians than is now the case, though the experience of what they may do in such work is already very considerable."

Lord Hobhouse said : " I am clear that the important matters mentioned above

can be better done by women In my
judgment we are, by our refusal to employ
women in public functions, guilty of a
waste of power, almost incredibly stupid.
There are vast fields of public work crying
out for labourers, and starved for want of
them.   There are vast numbers of women
ready and eager to help.   And yet we go
on appointing men too busy with other
affairs to attend to anything requiring
close detailed supervision, and rejecting
women who can give us what we want."

Mr. John G. Talbot, M.P., said on June
17, 1893 : "I value highly the presence
of ladies on each Board of Guardians.   I
am sure there are many branches of Poor-
Law Work in which their advice and
energy are eminently useful ; and I have
had great pleasure in serving with them
upon   more   than   one   such   Board   in
London."

Dr. T. H. Bridges, M.B., Inspector of
the Local Government Board, makes this
emphatic statement : "I should be glad
to see it recognised as a rule that a certain
proportion of every Board of Guardians

should be women . . . it is essential that the judgment of experienced women should be taken into account."

The Rev. Canon J. Erskine Clarke, formerly Chairman of the Wandsworth and Clapham Union, testifies : " From a long experience as a Poor-Law Guardian I am sure that there is a most useful work which Lady Guardians can do much better than men. No Board can quite satisfactorily discharge its difficult and various functions without the aid of Lady Guardians."

The Rev. Brooke Lambert, Guardian of Greenwich, Chairman of the Infirmary Committee, Greenwich Union, believes that : " Women are in their natural place on Boards of Guardians. It is my experience that the lack of women on Boards is a very serious hindrance to good work. I have advocated the election of women Guardians as a theory before I worked with them ; since I have seen them added to the Board of which I am a member, my opinion as to the value of their presence has been much strengthened."

THE HUMAN WOMAN

Mr. J. H. Allen, Ex-officio Guardian of St. Pancras, is " proud to say that during the last seven or eight years we have invariably had in St. Pancras three Lady Guardians on our Board. At first there was considerable opposition, but now their position is so universally recognised that in the event of an election taking place they are almost certain of being returned at the head of the poll. Over and over again I have heard the officials, both male and female, say they could not possibly now get on without the Lady Guardians, and the reason of this is obvious to any one who knows the many and complicate questions that arise in our Poor-Law establishments,which only women are competent to deal with. Personally, I can speak in the highest terms of their usefulness, and it would be a very evil day for us in St. Pancras, if from any unforeseen circumstances the ladies had to retire from our Board."

The Rt. Rev. Lord Bishop of Southwell says : . . . " Believing as I do that in workhouses, as in all other establishments

124

involving domestic economy, it is wise to appoint women in the management of such establishments."

Dr. Aschrotts, in his work on "The English Poor-Law System," affirms that : "The co-operation of women in Poor-Law administration has been everywhere found to be most useful. Sometimes particular branches have been entirely given over to them. . . . On all sides I have heard nothing but praise of the work of women as Guardians."

The Archbishop of Canterbury, in a letter to a member of the Council, says he is delighted to hear so good an account of the work of the Women's Local Government Society, with which he has the profoundest sympathy.

Lord Wolverhampton, President of the Local Government Board, in his reply to the Deputation of the Women's Liberal Federation, December 7, 1892, when he was the Rt. Hon. Henry H. Fowler, stated that he felt strongly that the services rendered by Women Guardians were of the greatest national importance, and he trusted that at the next election of Guardians in the forthcoming spring, there would be a great addition to the number of women on the Boards.

Mr. Balfour, Lords Courtney, Salisbury, Londonderry, and Kimberley have all raised their voices to give similar testimony, as to the usefulness of women on public bodies, and their utterances are on record.

It is not only as guardians of the Poor that men can be found to praise the public work of women, pæans of praise are raised by all intelligent, honest men who have worked on public bodies with women. Lord Reay, Chairman of the late London School Board, amongst many who have expressed equally favourable opinions, says : " To illustrate the vast amount of labour which this administration entails, I cannot do better than give a few typical instances of the work done by individual members of the Board. One member, a lady, is Vice-Chairman of one Principal Committee, a member of two ; Chairman

of three Sub-Committees, and a member
of ten. As Chairman of the Domestic
Subjects Sub-Committee, she has to deal
with the needlework taught in 441 Girls'
and in 82 Mixed Departments, with the
classes of Cookery, Laundry, and Housewifery in 333 centres. These classes
require constant watchfulness and development, as I know from the experience I
obtained in the Special Committee appointed to report on this work, over which
I presided. I consider that this duty alone
would constitute a sufficient task, but in
this member's case it forms only a part
of her manifold duties . . . She is . . .
Chairman of her Divisional Committee,
and she has fourteen schools under her
charge, all of which make demands upon
her time. . . . The amount of her correspondence is enormous, and it is only by
giving up her whole life to all these various
duties that the mandate can be discharged.
It is quite clear that no paid official could
be asked to undertake these duties, that
no Trade Union would allow any of its
members to work so much overtime, and

that it is only the sense of direct responsibility, that is created by the election of the Members of this Board, and in which they reap their chief, if not their only reward, which can account for so much devotion to duty. I could give a similar account of the work of other ladies on this Board, but my space will only allow me to give one specimen. *It should further be noted that much of the work described could only be done by a lady,* and that the exclusion of ladies would deal a fatal blow to the efficiency of this Board."

Now, in accordance with the invariable rule that I have formed, and notwithstanding the ample endorsement my own views receive at the hands of many able and eminent men, I carefully examine any adverse views expressed either in public or in private. Considerable service appears to have been unconsciously rendered to what is called the woman's cause,—although in the words of our greatest nineteenth-century poet :

" The woman's cause is man's, they rise or sink
Together, dwarfed or god-like, bond or free "—

by an article which appeared some time
ago in the *Nineteenth Century* commenting adversely on woman's public work.
The service rendered was by enabling one
to judge of the value of what we may
presume to be the best available argument
by which the opponents of the " Woman
Question " endeavour to demonstrate the
undesirability of women's co-operation in
public work. I quote an example of their
method of reasoning :—

"Woman's strength lies in having something to grant which can only be granted
to the favoured. . . . From this has resulted a different way of speaking to man
from the man's way of speaking to her ;
an unfair way, let us say, at once, if we
assume the point of view and the object
aimed at by both sexes to be the same.
And there has resulted, too, that woman
has prevailed to have it assumed as a social
axiom that the way shall be different, and
to have the sense of unfairness lost in the
sense of the objects of interest being different as between man and man and between woman and man. At this early

period of my remarks I can conceive a champion of woman's public appearances saying : 'Oh, but this is all so antediluvian. It is assuming the perpetuity of an old-fashioned relation. This old-fashioned relation is one of the very things we are incidentally going to destroy.' It is of no use to reply, 'Are you?' The other side will not regard the question as conclusive, and it is enough to call the attention of the impartial to the fact that the very women who wish to establish the right to every responsible public appearance are rather more than the old-fashioned women, precise upon the point of etiquette, rather more ready than the old-fashioned women to say, 'Oh, of course, he could not contradict a woman.' 'Of course, he could not say that to me, because I am a woman.'"

Now, I can understand the writer of the above being prepared to hear the " champion of woman's public appearances" demur at the amazing axioms dogmatically laid down as to " the objects of interest being different between man and man, and between man and woman."

But I absolutely deny the possibility of any intelligent " champion " doing so in the manner indicated. Neither before nor after the flood were the " objects of interest," nor the objects of intercourse, invariably different between men and women, and men and men, when the object of intercourse happened to turn on the common rights, the common progress, or the common aspirations of all human beings.

Then as to the statements contained in the end of the passage quoted, that " it is enough to call attention to the fact " that the " very women who wish to establish a right to every responsible public appearance are rather more unreasonable and illogical than any other kind," I would ask for whom is it enough ?—for the writer himself, or for the public for whom he writes ? That no woman who has ever held a responsible public position, or aspires to it, would indulge in the feeble sayings here attributed wholesale to her, I am equally ready to characterise as " fact," with more chance of being able to prove my facts, if it came to a test of evidence, than are our antagonists to prove theirs. Furthermore, I assert that in any discussion, either public or private, where men and women are thoroughly in earnest, and anxious to arrive at the truth, the sex bias is lost sight of. But it is not by dogmatic counter-assertions that I propose to confute the arguments of our would-be annihilators.

Let us examine exactly what it is that a gentleman, who constituted himself the spokesman of the Anti-Woman Party, fears. This gentleman says that certain relations exist between the sexes which are so fundamental that nothing will upset them. It may at once be conceded that whatever of value to the general good there is, in the established relations of the sexes, *will* endure, even when beneficial reforms have been introduced, which may tend to modify or vary certain existing relationships. It is, however, asserted that part of this fundamental relationship consists in an element, which makes it impossible for a mixed assembly to carry out a discussion in such a manner that it may reach its ripest fruition. A sweeping conclusion, which has been illustrated by "defying the man who has had a nice father and mother," to deliver the "deadly unapproachable serve" to a woman, "even to the professed lawn-tennis-playing woman," in a game of lawn-tennis. And the illuminating illustrator deduces from the supposed fact of this occurrence being an impossiblity, that the man's tongue will likewise be hindered from delivering an argument calculated to have on the mental plane the same effect that the "deadly serve" would have on the physical. In the first place, it may be as well to observe that the quality here held up for our admiration is not confined to any one sex. I venture to assert that the "professed lawn-tennis-playing woman" would be just as capable of exercising the same magnanimity to a boy or man smaller and less expert than herself, when dealing him a serve in a game of lawn-tennis. Inability to take unfair advantage even when allowed by the ordinary rules of the games of lawn-tennis or of life, is here implied; but generosity, and a sense of justice, and other virtues are not male characteristics only. Therefore, the fact that men do possess them is not an invulnerable argument against the possibility of women's usefulness in debate. But, even supposing that these characteristics were exclusively male (and it is not the first, nor the last, time that men, dealing antagonistically with women's public potentialities, have modestly assumed all the virtues likely to be called into play in public life to be so, or that they have based their arguments on that assumption), even then it is not easy to see how qualities of such sterling merit can fail to have a beneficial influence, however, wherever, and whenever employed.

In the second place, if the deliverance of a " deadly serve " in a game of lawn-tennis carried with it a beneficial result more far-reaching in its effect than the temporary discomfiture of the person to whom it was dealt, then in spite, or perhaps in consequence, of the " niceness " of his parents, a man would probably deliver it. For the analogy of the game of lawn-tennis

to be of any use, the result of the " deadly
serve," and the unrestrained freedom of
speech must, on their respective planes,
be of equal value in effect. If the man's
want of restraint result only in the petty
triumph of the moment in exposing some
flaw in the woman's arguments, then the
restraining influence which would prevent
such a triumph would be beneficial, and of
greater value to the sum of general good
than the small point that would otherwise have been gained to the man. If,
on the other hand, some real advance in
the progress of truth would be hindered,
through the man's restraint, then the ultimate benefit to the cause of truth should,
and, I think, *would*, have greater weight
with an intelligent man than the thought of
a possible temporary slur likely to be cast on
his " good taste." The question to be decided is not the possible inconvenience to
men, which is all this hypothesis would
suggest, likely to arise from a disturbance
of the balance established by themselves,
as to the relative attitude of the sexes in
the conduct of the world's affairs, but the

gain to Humanity generally likely to be
derived therefrom. A single possible consequence undesirable in itself cannot be
accepted, unconditionally, as a proof of
the general undesirability of the whole of
any given achievement. And the possible
need that may arise for men to have to
re-adjust their ideas as to the mutual relation of the sexes towards each other,
and towards the world at large, is not an
unmixed evil to the female mind, which
commodity, after all, does exist, and is
worthy of its share, its full share, and the
largest share it can command in directing
the affairs of the world. "Nature," according to our vague antagonists, hitherto
man's partisan in these matters, should be
trusted to see that such share is not in
excess of woman's merits !

With reference to women's appointments as Guardians of the Poor, the same
writer to whom I have already referred,
asked us to believe that their presence is
" more calculated to do harm by the
hampering of truth than their special
aptitudes for finding out certain facts of

public import could do good." Why a woman's presence on Boards of Guardians should necessarily " hamper truth," and what are the " special aptitudes" she is credited with we are not told, but such an expression of opinion does not appear to afford a contribution of any great value towards the elucidation of the subject under discussion. But to the practical usefulness of women on Boards of Guardians I can myself testify. The District Council on which I served for five years consisted of twenty-three members, two of whom were women, one a clergyman, two " squires," and the rest farmers. Three reforms have been introduced into the working of this Union : (1) the Brabazon employment scheme for the employment of aged or partially disabled paupers, who are unfit for the work of the institution ; (2) the board-ing-out system, and (3) the employment of "case papers." All three innovations were proposed by one or other of the two women-guardians, and carried with little or no opposition. I venture to assert that in this case the total amount of benefit gained by the influence of women, by the introduction of these reforms (which I am safe in saying would never have been established had the Board continued its existence composed of the same guardians as of old), more than counterbalances any possible loss resulting from the "stoppage of the free play of natural remark and contradiction" : which result, I am bound to admit, has been effected, if at all, then, as this prophet of evil feared would be the case, unobserved by the one woman-guardian for whom I am able to answer !

I purposely refrain from dwelling on the change for the better that has been effected in the management of the "House," and to which the inmates themselves testify with no uncertain voice, or from enlarging on the greater individual attention that each case now receives, because no sufficient evidence can be produced to show that it is necessarily the existence of women-guardians by which any improvement in these matters has been wrought ; but the three innovations I have mentioned as having been actually

established through their agency is a solid
fact. And this small rural Union is not
by any means an isolated, nor indeed by
very many the most worthy, example of
the improvements bearing witness to the
presence of women who have been elected
to serve as Guardians of the Poor.

On certain questions which came to a
division, my fellow woman-guardian and
myself did not invariably vote on the same
side, and the significance of this fact I
would like to emphasise, as it goes to prove
the improbability, nay, the impossibility of
there being any question, any subject, any
law requiring reform on which all women
would range themselves on one side, and
all men (to their honour be it said) on the
other. Therefore, in a mixed debate there
would still be opportunities afforded for
the interchange of that " rudeness " which
we have been told is " indispensable to the
real treatment of public questions," because
this " rudeness " could be employed by the
women among one another, or by the men
amongst themselves. If a man desired to
make some point in answer to a woman

opponent which involved the use of some
argument, calculated to risk for him the
loss of " favour " to gain which it has been
suggested all men's actions towards women
are governed by, he could, if with him
this consideration so far out-weighed any
mere thought of justice and truth, "instruct
a junior" or even a senior lady on the ·
same side, how to answer on the point
in question, and thus arm her with the
weapon which he is himself afraid to use.
But the absurdity of the whole contention
should be sufficiently obvious, divesting its
supporter, as it does, of any sign of possess-
ing a sense of proportion. For he made
no attempt to show that any subject under
discussion would not be more widely, more
thoroughly, more comprehensively discussed, if women brought their point of
view to bear upon the discussion, except
by an endeavour to prove that their
presence would be instrumental in pre-
venting the *men* from ventilating their
views in the freest manner and to the
greatest possible extent. The motive
assigned which causes their reticence is

not, be it observed, the fear of in any way
hindering the progress of truth, but the
fear of trespassing against that unwritten
code of chivalry, and thereby doing *themselves* a temporary injury, judged, not by
the standard of an exalted modern ideal,
but by the "radical relations of man to
woman" which have been "settled by
nature long ago!"

So obvious does the inevitable gain to
public life that women's co-operation
would afford appear, that one may be sure
that any objection thereto is based on
purely selfish or self-seeking principles.
One is therefore not surprised to find such
words as these: "So super-eminent is
the influence of women over men *that we
must protect ourselves*." This is the key-
note to all such arguments. The desire is
avowedly not to advocate the cause of
human progress generally, but to emphasise
the conflicting interests existing, in imagination, between men and women; and in
women's encroachment on the sphere of
public life, it is not a possible all-round
gain, but *merely* an encroachment on men's

present power that is anticipated. The influence of women from which men require to " protect themselves " must be an evil one. This amounts to an admission that the qualities awakened by women in men are far from being the noble, generous characteristics that we are invited to believe, but of so pernicious a character as to make it impossible for women to cooperate with men in public life. We have been given to understand that the influence over men described as "fascination" evokes qualities in man which rob him of his reasoning powers and of his debating powers—in fact, that his sense of sex is too strong to enable him to forget it if a woman joins in a debate in which he is taking part. And for this reason a woman is to be debarred from taking her possible share in public work on the ground that it would, in consequence of men's insuperable instincts, have disastrous results !

One writer, I remember, based his objection to women taking part in public life on the ground of duty, and as one of those who " respected women much, but loved their country more." But the phrase failed to inspire one with the admiration for which the writer was bidding, or with a belief in the genuineness of "his respect," but seemed rather to savour of cant, for he was not ashamed subsequently to deliver himself of the cheapest form of sneer traceable in the words : "and silent ones [women] *where found.*" Have we not all known instances in public and private life where women have shown that they realise that in certain matters, "Silence is most noble," and have nobly kept that silence "to the end"?

Let the arm still be restrained from the deliverance of a "deadly ball" to a weaker opponent on the lawn-tennis ground, and let the tongue still be withheld from uttering vituperative recriminations on the higher field of Reason, that the one may be employed with keener power in succouring the weak and oppressed, and the other directed with greater force against the unrighteous advocacy of injustice.

All objections to this obviously logical standpoint usually takes one of two forms.

143

THE HUMAN WOMAN

Men of one class of mind base their objection to women serving their fellow-beings in a public capacity, on the ground of their " reverence and admiration " for women. " I do not like to think of women mixing in the strife and turmoil of public life," they will say. Women are to them " sacred, tender creatures designed to minister to the highest qualities of men," their gift for which " ministry " would be tarnished and impaired should they " emerge from the sacred precincts of home life." Men of another stamp base their objection frankly on their belief in women's general incapacity. They contend that women are not perfect, and that consequently they may make mistakes, that they are not angels but human beings. That they are, in a word, women. It is true that perfection is not claimed—we are modestly assured—for men, but then it is better to stick to the evils that we know than to fly to others that we know not of. All such " arguments " are dreary and dispiriting. Those who make use of them appear to me only half human and not endowed with all the qualities derived from a fully-developed human brain. It is these who produce the *androphobia* which causes the rather ferocious outbursts of "anti - man - ism" and anti-maternity that Mrs. Caird and Madame Sarah Grand and their followers occasionally indulge in. But these illogical anti-*féministe* arguments no more represent virile male thought than what I have called "anti-man-ism" and *androphobia* represent the true woman's movement.

It is, however, often thought that to suggest a woman as Speaker of the House of Commons, for instance, has reduced the question of Women in Assemblies to its last absurdity. I was speaking to a well-known public man on the subject of woman's capability for any high office : I mentioned the name of a certain lady well known as a supporter of the women's movement, widow of a cabinet-minister who owed more than usual, owing to circumstances, to his wife's help. My friend unhesitatingly and ungrudgingly admitted at once that he considered her admirably fitted for many posts, and himself volunteered the office of Speaker as one which he would feel great confidence in her ability to fulfil. I have had the privilege of sitting on Committees with her myself when she has acted as chairman. The quiet authoritative manner, with all absence of bombast or unnecessary red tape, is a sure indication of power. The serene consciousness of adequate knowledge, together with the willing deference to the sincerely expressed opinion of others, all go to inspire that confidence without which no authority can be exercised. I am quite willing to admit that the lady I have in my mind is an exceptional woman. But is it to be supposed that every man is capable of becoming Speaker, or of filling any other high office of State, or will it be acknowledged that amongst the women likely to be candidates for the office, the proportion of able persons would be very much greater than amongst men aspiring to the same positions? A woman who, in spite of the competition, in spite of the prejudice she will have to overcome, shall actually have been elected to such a post is very unlikely to prove incompetent or a failure, and the sex disability merely has the effect of limiting the choice amongst the persons most capable of serving their country in any capacity. It has the effect, as it has had in the past, of stunting the development of abilities which may be exceptionally marked in certain individuals, if those individuals happen to be women, because there is no reason for their cultivation. The development of the race as a whole is thus thwarted and atrophied. It will not, I hope, be thought that I am making the fatuous suggestion that the particular lady I have in my mind, or any other, could adequately fulfil all the arduous duties of a Speaker without having by perseverance and training acquired all the requisite knowledge of the intricacies and subtleties of Parliamentary procedure; I merely suggest that having had the opportunity of assimilating them, which industry and ordinary intelligence would enable an individual to do, the other essential qualities, also necessary to the office which cannot be acquired, such as tact, judgment, and a wide, fair-minded impartiality together with a deep-seated sense of proportion belong to some women as well, and are not characteristics by which the male sex can be easily and definitely distinguished. There are some people who see no reason to change the positively *stupid* arrangement at present existing, because through its perpetuation, a certain number of men and women suffer neither inconvenience, loss, nor general discredit in any of the various commonplace circumstances of current life that constitute the whole of life for most of them. Clearly then, thinking women cannot wait, are not indeed waiting until abstract justice alone is powerful enough to govern the action of those in authority. This is the moment, however, above all others, when they must rouse themselves, and by obtaining justice for themselves and their fellow-women, earn the lasting gratitude of humanity, by the benefits that will thereby inevitably accrue to it.

I firmly believe that at some future

time the existing generation of men and women will look back with amazement and incredulity at the one-sided character of human activities, as we now look back at some striking condition of the human race, the hidden pages of which the researches of archæology, biology, anthropology, or geology are able to reveal to us. I believe it to be as true that those whom God has joined it is not within the power of man to put asunder, as it is true that the destiny of the human race cannot eventually be prevented from fulfilling itself by the feeble machinations of facts or factions. The responsibility is, nevertheless, great in those who willingly hinder its development, either through ignorance, prejudice, or fear, whether these qualities assume the self-glorifying attributes of caution, stability, or a deluded sense of competence. It is not given to all to be prophets and seers, but the race of those who cry " go up, bald head " when they do make their appearance (and with less excuse, for the race is now more nearly grown up), is not yet extinct, and as surely will the same fate overtake them in this generation.

VII

WOMEN'S NEWSPAPERS

An article under the heading of "Women's Progress and Women's Press" in the *Albany Review* has given me the peg for which I was seeking on which to hang the subject of Women's Newspapers, because it offers an insight into the views of those who are anxious to find opportunities whereon to base their condemnation of the Women's Movement by misconstruing actual facts into an argument in favour of their own preconceived opinions. The writer, who signs himself X, begins his article by asking his readers to believe that after having addressed a series of "deferential and dispassionate inquiries" to some of the "leaders of the Women's Suffrage Movement," he is in the satisfactory position of "knowing the main grounds" upon which the demand for the concession of the suffrage is made.

These he enumerates by "speaking roughly" under three heads, and proceeds to show that this demand is based upon : (1) complete ignorance of modern political history : (2) absence of logic in the female mind : (3) inordinate sex-vanity. Their ignorance of modern political history is shown in "the old argument about taxation and representation going hand in hand." Now, if any person, a leader or an ordinary man or woman, ever made the assertion that taxation and representation invariably *did* go together (or hand in hand as X thinks he more elegantly expresses it), then I think they must not only be ignorant of "political history" but strangely ignorant of the very subject on which this "series of deferential and dispassionate inquiries" were being made. If, however, these "leaders" had told this deferential and dispassionate inquirer that one fundamental axiom, I do not say of Liberalism, but of the Liberal party, had always been that taxation and representation *should* go together, then she would only have been stating a fact so well known that the

inquirer might almost have been able
to deduce the " answer " for himself, without troubling the " leaders " to retail to him
so elementary a piece of common knowledge.   These   same   leaders,   however,
show their " want of logic " by also telling
this inquiring gentleman " that since men
have the vote, women ought to have it."
What they probably told him (only perhaps the phrase was too long for him to
remember it in its entirety) was that all
the reasons that made the vote the desired
and desirable possession of men, applied
equally to women.   It will take more
than a trite sneer at " women's logic " to
prove that this is not so.   But of the
third " reason " our inquirer gives—that
is, women's belief in " the incontestable,
unshakable superiority of the female sex."
I may say that during all the years I have
worked, spoken, and written in favour of
the enfranchisement of women, not only
have I never urged such a silly proposition
myself, but I have never heard any person,
man   or   woman,   advocating   Women's
Suffrage, make use of any " argument " re-

motely approaching such a feeble, futile
contention. This dispassionate, earnest
seeker after information goes on to assert
that " This ' truth,' with its natural corollary of Man's Inferiority, is held, as I have
indicated, with absolute, unshakable, and
most passionate unanimity by all sections
alike." There is more of this sort of
thing, but the feelings he is filled with in
view of his belief in this being " the
absolute, unshakable, and most passionate
opinion of women of all sections of the
Women's Suffrage Movement" about themselves and each other, are really not interesting enough to quote. But the passage
I have quoted seems to me a little over in-
flated : anything that is " absolute " must
be unshakable. If Mr. X had made
even an elementary study of philosophical
" grammar" he would not make so free
with the use of the word " absolute," or
think it gained strength by the subsequent
addition of " unshakable " and " most
passionate." But, curiously enough, I
attended a " debate " on Women's Suffrage
only a few days ago, and one of the
" opposers " of the question based his

objection to women having the vote on
the manifestation of the supreme contempt held for their own sex by women
suffragists. This he "proved" by the
suffragist literature wherein he con-
tended that what should be the most
sacred beings on earth—their mothers and
grandmothers—were scorned as persons
holding obsolete and degrading views
of life. A lady followed who tried to explain that all the pamphlet in question
suggested was that the ideals held up
in fiction for our admiration formerly had
been superseded in modern literature;
that the heroines no longer "swooned"
at every rough word, or surmounted a
difficult situation by fainting into the arms
of either the hero or her female friends;
that the "Eugenic Society" held up to
ridicule the supposed chivalry of the
valiant suitor who espoused the consump-
tive charity-girl, and raised innumerable
offspring from so contaminated a source;
and that the self-reliant, independent
modern maiden was more worthy of
admiration than her clinging, cringing,
whimpering forerunner.

Indeed, the variety of criticisms founded
upon diametrically opposing contentions
affords a sort of amused wonderment to
those who have seriously studied the
Woman's Movement. Our opponents
lay bare the barrenness of their ground,
and show how little, how superlatively
little, knowledge or thought seems to be
considered enough for those who gaily
undertake a " reasoned " demonstration
of " Woman's unfitness for the demand
she is making." Mr. X, however,
seems to base his "reasoning" on the
terrible exposition of women's crude incompetence, as revealed by the women's
newspapers of to-day. Now, it has perhaps not occurred to him that these papers
are initiated, financed, and chiefly staffed
by males. It is the male idea of women's
needs, as supplied by the newspapers that
are offered to them, and on this subject I
shall have a word to say later.

By a curious coincidence a few days ago
a lady, who has been entrusted with the
editorship of a few pages in a little three-
penny monthly paper, called on me by

appointment to ask my help and advice
in a scheme that she was eager to carry
out. She felt keenly on the subject of the
uselessness and the frivolity of the ordinary
women's journals, and she wished, in as
attractive and disarming a way as possible,
gradually to try to introduce into the
part of the paper for which she was
responsible, some wider, higher ideas,
than fashion and gossip. She explained
to me quite frankly that in the large
class of women amongst whom her newspaper was circulated, they regarded the
subject of Women's Suffrage as "not quite
nice." She assured me that it was their
fixed idea that their male relations would
not approve of women taking an interest
in anything beyond their dress, their
home, their babies, and their little social
entertainments. This lady hoped that
her paper might be the means of doing a
certain amount of insidious propagandist
work, and it was in this effort that she
hoped to enlist my sympathy and support.
I quote this actual and recent experience
of mine, as it seems to be a direct answer

to the indictment delivered by Mr. X in his comments on the futility and frivolity of the aims of women journalists. "I shall have to move cautiously," this particular propagandist explained to me—"because it was not for this kind of work that I was engaged as sub-editor, and I may be told that it is not the kind of work that is wanted from me." And yet Mr. X calmly asserts that "Educated women have abundant opportunities in their own Press to exhibit the high reformatory qualities that they promise to exercise in politics." He thinks, too, that "no one conversant with the actual condition of things will contest" his statements. We shall see.

Mr. X, furthermore, takes women to task for not realising how immensely greater their present power is than any power the vote could bring would be. "What, after all," he asks, "are the powers and performances of Government compared to the enormous power for good or evil of an absolutely free newspaper Press?" What this gentleman's

157

idea of an "absolutely free" Press is I am not in a position to gather from his article, but again the word "absolutely" of which he is very fond, and of which he apparently does not recognise the significance, is not the right word wherewith to characterise the existing "freedom" of the Press as far as the public is concerned. I have known of controversies carried on in the *Times* newspaper and the *Spectator* on women's subjects where letters controverting the opinions and assertions contained in these publications have been refused admittance, while others upholding and supporting their own views have been inserted.

The public, and especially women, have not that "absolutely free" access to the columns of the newspapers that are widely read, which would make the ventilation of their views the obvious and easy source of power for moulding public opinion, which we are invited to believe is the glorious possession of women, that through ignorance, indolence, or indifference they refuse to avail themselves of.

NEWSPAPERS FOR WOMEN

The spectacle of a daily paper changing its policy in a single night is not unknown to observers of our wonderful "free Press." Had women unlimited funds at their disposal, the phenomenon of a frankly antagonistic journal becoming suddenly enthusiastically favourable to their demands, might also be observed. These vehicles of public opinion are to be bought and sold like any other commodity, and the highest bidder for this privilege of freedom of expression is not necessarily the most worthy. The economic position of women is not taken into account when they are twitted with their apparent sluggishness in failing to avail themselves of the existing privileges which they are held so abundantly to possess.

It is unfortunately too true that this one-sex-represented Press is "free" to pick and choose what it considers of interest to the public whose opinion it is undertaking to form. Hence, anything in the Woman's Movement that is considered sufficiently sensational or discreditable is duly "reported," exaggerated, and noticed at considerable length. But the well-weighed words of wisdom enunciated at large representative public meetings organised by women pass wholly unnoticed, and the existence of the gatherings themselves is more often than not entirely ignored.

At a debate recently held in one of the well-known debating clubs in London, women's newspapers were discussed. The subject called forth a good deal of violent condemnation of most of the existing " Ladies' papers," in a manner quite calculated to satisfy those most eager to condemn. They were frivolous and low-toned, they represented neither literature nor art ; moreover, they turned the heads of the working-girl by imbuing her with a love of cheap finery, and cheap romance. Extracts were read from some of these papers, and the matter selected was certainly not edifying.

I found myself agreeing with most of what was said, as, so far as I could make out, did all the other people present. So,

out of a spirit of perversity, I tried to
raise a few arguments in defence of the
condemned publications. These papers,
I ventured to say, afforded recreation to
the working-girls ; if they were not reading them, they might be doing something
worse. After all, I said, they apparently
gave pleasure—and pleasure itself had a
certain intrinsic value on this drear earth.
This tentative view of mine subsequently
received support from Mr. Thomas
Holmes, the well-known London police-
court missionary and himself an author,
who has, to quote the *Westminster Gazette*
—" A Word for the ' Penny Dreadful.' "

Mr. Holmes was not able to recall in
all his experience a case where crime had
resulted from the mere reading by boys of
what are known as blood-and-thunder
stories :

" The penny dreadful, whatever else it
may be, does at least preserve a continuity
of thought, a concentration of mind.
Again, what do I find among many of
these poor London working-girls ? I find
them revelling in novelettes where the

chaste and beautiful housemaid comes off
triumphant and marries a dashing lord.
We may laugh at such literature as ridiculous, but it is really beneficial to those
girls. It takes them to a world other than
their own, and there is this to be said for
it, that the villain and the criminal always
get punished, while virtue always has its
reward."

"That is a good lesson in life," added
Mr. Holmes, "however it may be brought
home."

But in the club debate this did not do
at all. What! uphold the acquisition of
ill-gotten gain by exploiting the weaknesses and worst characteristics of those
who might be raised and elevated by the
same means? I succumbed, and owned
my defeat, and now I am quite prepared
to take up the cudgels against the side I
had feebly tried to defend.

There are, I believe, about fifty-five
newspapers for women, girls, and children,
twelve of which are registered as "Ladies'
papers" all more or less concerning dress,
and having, I suppose, in each some story

either complete or in a serial, wherein the
wicked baronet or the godless earl wins
the young affections of the beautiful and
honest maiden and then deserts her.
Barons, viscounts, and dukes, when they
exist, are generally respectable, and sometimes they succour the distressed damsel,
but a marquis is an unknown quantity.

These fifty-five papers, no doubt, supply
a demand or they would not exist, and the
question is, how is their influence to be
mitigated ? It would be difficult to find
some philanthropist who could be induced
to buy up all the papers as they appear, so
that none should fall into hands which
would be soiled by their contagious touch.
Perhaps a better way would be to start
some new ones, the tone of which would
be so lofty and electrically educative that
most of those now existing would find no
sale, and so die a natural death.

Now, it must have been some idea of
this kind that induced Lord Northcliffe
to start the *Daily Mirror*. When, however, an attempt is made to supply "a
long-felt want," and the attempt fails,

either the want did not exist, or the right method was not adopted.

Now that the *Daily Mirror* has taken its place, side by side, with a host of other half-penny publications not professing to minister to the needs of one sex more than to the other, it may be amusing, and even interesting and profitable to recall the pomp and show which heralded its first appearance, and to analyse what this reputed want was, which it set itself so painstakingly to fill. Let us examine this experienced male newspaper proprietor's views of " women's needs " and the supposed measure of its fulfilment.

The want was a daily paper where women would be " able to find news concerning all the interests of their lives," which they were assured, whether they knew it or not, they had never been able to find elsewhere.

The method by which this want was to be met was duly set forth. First of all there were alluring advertisements that must have made the mouths of expectant womankind to water prodigiously ; but the day dawned at last when woman came into her own. There, before her was *The Paper*, and under the head of " *Daily Mirror* Departments" the following list was paraded :—

1. Women's employment   [No extra clauses.]
2. Women's work in the field of religion.
3. Dress of the day.   [With nine subdivisions.]
4. The medicine cupboard.—How to treat emergencies ; simple ailments in the nursery, &c.
5. The nursery.   [Two subdivisions only.]
6. Outdoor gardening
7. Indoor gardening.
8. Pets for pleasure and for profit.
9. Indoor games. Bridge, &c. [*Sic.*]
10. The jewel box.
11. Women's sports and pastimes.
12. Physical exercises.
13. The hygiene of the home
14. Flowers for the table and the house.
15. The appointments for the dinner-table.
16. The house beautiful.
17. Old lace, old china, and old silver.
18. The cult of beauty.—The complexion, the hair, manicure, &c.
19. Educational subjects —Schools for boys and girls , school outfits.
20. Photography.

Twenty "Departments," and where was the kitchen ?—according to the autocratic

THE HUMAN WOMAN

Emperor of the Germans one-third of the whole of woman's life.

But not only cookery and politics apparently, but neither the drama, literature, art, science, nor sociology have any place in "Woman's Daily Life." And yet on the same page under the heading " Practical side of the *Daily Mirror*," we had the following promises : " As day passes day readers of the *Daily Mirror* will find that *all* the varied interests of womankind receive their *due* share of attention." (The italics are mine.)

Immediately under this, and in order, we suppose, to give the paper a cosmopolitan flavour was an article in French by a Frenchman. In this we were definitely reassured that we should not be troubled with politics. I translate the following gems culled from this article : " What a happy and useful thought this inception of the *Daily Mirror !* The birth of a daily journal of a kind, that while avoiding politics, seeks solely to instruct and to amuse woman is an event of the highest importance—the

progress, the future of this infant pro-
digy will be followed with much interest by a great number of French
women."

" Why ? " . . .

" Firstly, because it concerns itself above
all with what women in general, and
French women in particular, *hold most
dear, La Mode*."

Now, in holding these quotations up to
receive their just share of ridicule, I do
not wish it to be supposed that I pose
as a person who thinks that the *toilette*
should have no place at all in a woman's
existence—on the contrary, I consider an
ostentatious disregard of fashion as foolish
as a slavish adherence to its decrees. Did
not Marcus Aurelius point out that the
curled and scented fop of Rome was
nearer to the right path than the slovenly
youth who paraded the neglect of his
personal appearance under a mistaken
notion that it was the sign of the cynic ?
But there is a wide margin between the
legitimate care of the person, be it that
of male or female, involving even æsthetic

167

considerations due to a proper pride in one's appearance, and the wholly unjustifiable absorption advocated in the paragraphs cited above. It is against the latter view that I enter my protest. It is this paltry view of " Woman's Sphere " that prompts the writing, and induces the toleration of the methods displayed by the male writer on dress. In the first article on this ubiquitous subject in the same issue of the wonderful publication to which I have referred, the writer begins by recommending daintiness in a certain feminine undergarment, " because nothing impresses mere man more favourably than a discreet glimpse thereof ! "

One more quotation from the same sheet and I have done. After mentioning Shakespeare's " unhappy union " our paragraphist continues—" But she (Shakespeare's wife) inspired her daughters with affection, and if there were sad chapters in the home life at Stratford, what woman that ever lived, we may well ask, could have completely responded to the master mind of the human race ? "

NEWSPAPERS FOR WOMEN

It was this kind of " literature " for which women were asked to be deeply grateful—which was going to fill a daily want in their lives !

Now a curious thing happened : it took, I believe, a storm-tossed fortnight before this paper rode for a fall and settled down to its present state of, I am told, widely-circulating, but non-specialised journalistic achievement. On the second day, however, there appeared in the paper itself many letters bearing more or less distinguished signatures from ladies professing to feel great gratification at the compliment bestowed on the female sex ; the compliment of considering it worthy of having one daily newspaper devoted exclusively to its members. Some of the writers of these letters manifested a most touching and becoming humility and a deep sense of gratitude for so signal a favour.

Well, I have briefly hinted at the fate that befell this much-advertised venture which was warranted to fill a " long-felt want."

The same fate will always attend any

venture that seeks artificially to differen-
tiate between the sexes. Artificially, I say :
no more useful end would be served by
passing a law ensuring that " only strong-
armed persons should be blacksmiths,"
than would be served by passing a law
enacting that " males should occasionally
bear children."

The conclusion seems inevitable that
the class to which the *Daily Mirror*
was meant to appeal have what they want
in other daily papers. The class which
keeps alive these other little " rags " are
already supplied and take their nauseating
potions in monthly, weekly, or in daily
draughts. There is, curiously enough,
one male fashion-paper called, I believe,
The Tailor and Cutter.[1] It is difficult
to see how even this one appeal to the
" dressy " portion of the male population
finds enough subscribers to keep it going.
Who or what reads it I do not profess to
know, and although I have never seen the

[1] Since writing the above I have been informed that there
are two or three other publications devoted to the description
of male attire But I presume that they are merely for
circulation " in the trade "

paper, I know that it exists, by sometimes seeing extracts quoted from its pages in the *Westminster Gazette*.

I think this proportion of 1 to 55 must be taken as showing the male estimate of the greater appreciation of *chiffons* in women than in men.

The complaint of my club debaters was, however, that this element was fostered and encouraged in women by the wicked newspaper-proprietor. But I can only suggest one remedy—the universal panacea for both readers and writers, and for all troubles, mental, moral, and physical, and that is *education*, on the right moral basis.

VIII

THE FREEDOM OF WOMEN

A PAMPHLET was recently published under the somewhat grandiloquent, but misleading title of "'The Freedom of Women,' by Ethel B. Harrison." The publishers have apparently thought it necessary to supplement this by explanatory headlines printed above the title, "'Against Female Suffrage,' by Mrs. Frederic Harrison." It is a perfectly harmless, inoffensive little volume of some fifty pages. I say inoffensive advisedly, because some anti-suffrage "literature" is anything but inoffensive. In the preface Mrs. Harrison says that those who are "fighting with sincerity and devotion" for Women's enfranchisement "have made the capital blunder of despising the opinions of the women who are against them." I confess that, for my part, it is true that the opinions that I have heard expressed by anti-suffrage women do not seem to me

172

to be respectworthy. With every desire to respect the writer of the anti-Suffrage pamphlet that I have referred to, I cannot pretend to feel any respect for the opinions expressed therein. When, however, I was lately asked to write a short paper in favour of the vote being extended to women I thought I could not do better than examine the arguments put forth in the latest anti-suffrage effort that has been thought worthy of publication, and endeavour to refute the reasons the opponents of the movement think it worth while to advance.

I will confess, too, at once that the perusal of a pamphlet of this kind does more to strengthen my convictions and arouse my enthusiasm than some of the suffrage meetings that I have attended.

Now, Mrs. Harrison begins her arguments by the old method of setting up a bogey, then proceeding to knock it down with much satisfaction. For instance, she divides her first chapter on " Fallacies " into the three heads : " That women are a separate class." " That women are not citizens." "That the interests of the sexes are antagonistic." She has devoted three pages to showing that women are not a class. Now, personally, I cannot imagine any one being so stupid, seeing how classes are divided, as to dispute the self-evident fact that there are women in all classes, that they belong to the one in which they find themselves, and not to a separate class formed by all women. In a speech this year I took occasion to point out that one reason for *not* pursuing the methods resorted to by men to obtain enfranchisement was that in every agitation carried on by men for the extention of the franchise, a class conflict was involved, which in the demand that women are making is wholly absent. Whether it has been unadvisedly maintained that women are a class or not, does not seem to me to bear in the remotest possible way on whether women should have a vote or not, and to prove that it has been said, and to prove that it is not so, are questions altogether beside the mark.

Mrs. Harrison's next contention is that

174

women have a right to be called citizens
in their present unenfranchised condition.
She seems to think that if she can justify
women in patting themselves on the back,
and preening themselves on being entitled
to the epithet " citizen," that they have
no further grievance, and that once this
appellative right is established, any other
sinks into insignificance. An academic
argument round and about the meaning
of the word " citizen " does not seem to
me to bear with any particular lucidity on
the question of whether they would be in a
better position to fulfil the duties of citizenship, if they were represented in the public
Parliament of their country, which is called
and supposed to be a representative body.

The third fallacy or bogey that Mrs.
Harrison sets up is that the " interests of
the sexes are antagonistic." Now, Mrs.
Harrison takes five pages to say what can
be said in a single phrase—that is, that no
properly balanced intelligent and educated
man or woman could fail to be aware that
the interests of all human beings, whether
men or women, are identical. And herein,

175

to my mind, lies the strongest argument
in favour of Women's Suffrage. Mrs.
Harrison says : " The injustice of men,
the brutality of men, the selfishness of men,
are insisted upon with so much vehemence,
and in such terms as to make the reader
wonder from what world such experiences
can have been gained." It occurs to me,
too, to wonder where Mrs. Harrison has
obtained her propagandist literature, which
she seems to have digested with much
avidity. I am happy to say I have not
seen it, but then perhaps I only read my
own sayings on the subject ! It is safe to
say that Mrs. Harrison has not culled her
gems from these. No, my reason for believing in the necessity of a vote, from the
very fact that men's and women's interests
are identical is not based on a belief in
men's injustice, brutality, or selfishness at
all, but merely in their inadequacy and
incompetence. And I do not mean
this in any way offensively, I mean that
as in the beginning the legend has it
that, " man and woman created he him "
(man), so since the human being has be-

come differentiated into man and woman, it requires the co-operation of men and women to work the affairs of State for the lives that it has required their joint efforts to produce.

Because a few foolish women may be found who will heap abuse on the whole race that happen to turn out to be males, or some equally foolish men are to be found who will alternately pedestalise or vilify the whole feminine creation, is that any reason for not looking soberly and steadfastly into the claim that women are now making in the name of reason, justice, and common-sense ?

In her next chapter Mrs. Harrison rubs in the well-worn phrases concerning women's failure to achieve greatness. But in war which may be considered exclusively man's department, the one name that stands out supreme in the annals of history is a woman's. Mrs. Harrison asserts that " in music, painting, and literature women's opportunities have long been equal to men's." I question the accuracy of this remark. Mary Somerville, who, as I took occasion to remark before, now has a bust in the Royal Institution, had to hide her studies under some needlework, as they were considered unwomanly. And who can say how many geniuses have had their potentialities nipped in the bud by like treatment. Mrs. Harrison proceeds to quote Mrs. Eddy as the one woman credited with founding a religion. She, however, goes on to say that " Mrs. Eddy has become an almost mythical personage ; it is highly problematical how much of the initiation of Christian Science belongs to her, how much to her adroit and clever lieutentants by whom she is surrounded." If this is to be an argument against the enduring influence of women, we may ask how much the rites and practices of Christianity and Buddhism resemble the religion practised and preached by the founders of either ? But this argument of women's achievements does not bear any more on the subject of the vote than the other considerations put up for the purpose of demolishing them I prefer to have this particular kind of argument advanced by a woman than by a man, for one remarks that the men who dwell upon women's inferiority are generally sorry specimens of humanity themselves, and cling to the accidental and supposed superiority that their sex gives them, perhaps being fully aware that in this accident alone lies the only claim to the superiority of which they boast. The man a schoolboy would describe as " an awfully decent chap," does not use that kind of argument.

Mrs. Harrison cites all the advantages men's labour gives to women in the arduous and dangerous occupations in which women have no share. I suppose the poor women who lose their health, senses, limbs, and sometimes their lives, in some of the " dangerous trades " in which they are miserably employed and shamefully underpaid, are not worthy of her consideration, so for the moment we will leave them there, not reckoned with and unrequited. " All this," she says, " is a free gift from men to women," and " is not repaid by the contribution of children to the community, because children are woman's crown of glory ! " "Her contribution is so unique in character that

179

it has no analogy with any other human
contribution to the race." "It would
seem to follow," she adds, "that as she is
free from other heavy burdens and responsibilities she should leave men free to conduct *them* without interference on her part."

I am not quite clear to what the " them "
refers, but I suppose to " other heavy
burdens and responsibilities." Now this
seems to be the stumbling-block of the
anti-suffragists. Men are not to be " in-
terfered " with. Why woman's share of
representation should be interference and
not co-operation I do not know, and have
never been able to see. In one breath we
are told that men's and women's interests
are identical, and in the next we are im-
plored to " allow men to do things in their
own way " without interfering with them.

But again, *is* childbearing the only
office that women perform for the State ?
Now although all mothers are women,
all women are not mothers, and does Mrs.
Harrison seriously believe that except as
childbearers women perform no service
to the State ? She forgets the important
and perhaps sad fact that 82 per cent.

of all the women in this country are wage-earners, and of the 18 per cent. that remain many give their services in public and in private to the extent that the sudden suspension of their work would mean chaos and dislocation of the gravest kind.

Mrs. Harrison reiterates the wearisome ineptitude that women have no " inherited aptitude" for certain things. Must we at this time of day remind her again of interlocked heredity, and ask her to recognise the very simple fact that boys inherit characteristics, aptitudes, and everything else from their mothers, as much, if not more than from their fathers ? Napoleon in choosing his officers is supposed to have said : " Show me first their mothers." Girls too equally inherit from both parents and not only from their mothers.

Mrs. Harrison says, " Work is never the first object in a woman's heart. She is also more liable to break down than the average man." Now I cannot pretend to this universal insight into a woman's heart, but I suppose that Mrs. Harrison is quite sure that the first object in a man's heart is always work. And I leave her in possession of her unique knowledge without venturing to contradict it. But *Mr.* Frederic Harrison, whom we presume to be the husband of the lady quoted, seems to be in marked disagreement with her on this point, for he says in one of his essays, " In qualities of constant movement, in passive endurance, in perseverance, in keenness of pursuit, in industriousness, in love of creating, of being busy rather than idle . . . it is a commonplace to acknowledge women to be our superiors." [1] But that the average woman is more liable to " break down " than the average man, I distinctly and emphatically deny. M. Bloch in his admirable book, "The Future of War," says : " In two weeks' time after the French Army is mobilised, it is the expectation of the best authorities that they would have 100,000 men in hospital, even if never a shot has been fired ; " and in the latest war in South Africa in our own army, in June 1900, deaths from diseases amounted to nearly 4000, and those killed in action or from wounds received in battle was considerably under 3000. Again, of the

[1] " Realities and Ideals," p. 74

17,000 sent home as incapable of service 12,000 were returned as sick and less than 4000 as wounded.[1] When an argument is based on woman's liability to " break down " let us, in the name of common-sense, not delude ourselves into supposing that men are any freer from the ills the flesh is heir to than are women.

Now with every word that Mrs. Harrison says as to the advisability of women forming Unions in self-protection, I am in profound agreement, but when she goes on to assert that to these women the vote would not be an asset, I can only ask her to look at the difference in the position of the man in the labour market since his acquisition of the vote and before, whereas as Mr. Sidney Webb says, women's wages remain at the same level as in their grand-mother's days.

Further on I come across a phrase to which I have appended a short marginal note : Mrs. Harrison asks " If man is so dangerous a thing as these ladies tell us, it is the wives, mothers," &c., &c. My query in the margin simply asks, " Which ladies? "

[1] See p. 88.

Of "these ladies" whose imbecilities are again and again quoted as being "the leaders" and "the movement," I simply say, "I know them not," and their utterances seem to me to be neither worth reading nor worth repeating. I at least have tried, in taking Mrs. Frederic Harrison as my text, to keep to a higher level.

A whole chapter is devoted to the actual laws that are said to be unjust to men. I offer this as the solution of so extraordinary a phenomenon : all these so-called advantages to women were made by men self-protectively, owing to women's economic position, and not, I fear, out of generosity. They are merely instances of man preying on man through the woman. Let any candid lawyer be asked whether this is not a perfectly accurate description of all the so-called advantages over men that women derive from a few of the existing laws.[1]

Then we come to a chapter on "the family." And I take great pleasure in quoting a whole sentence with which I find myself in absolute agreement. "No sane person can deny that men and women

[1] See p 194.

are different, for Nature has made them so.
It is only in combination as a group—father,
mother, child—that they reach completion;
it is only thus in the effort for the rearing
of children for the race that they best develop." Now, my belief in the truth of
this contention is my chief reason for
believing in the necessity for removing the
sex-disability, if this "completion" is to
take place in its highest sense, if "the
effort to rear children for the race" is to
be the joint work of both parents, then no
laws affecting the home, the education,
the responsibility of the parent, *can* be
properly initiated or properly carried out
without woman taking her share in the
councils of the nation.

But, alas, after the paragraph with which
I expressed agreement come the old
dreary platitudes about the "division of
labour"—"the man going abroad to do
and earn and the woman remaining in the
home." In the first place, the woman has
already been "driven from her home"
into the labour market. That fact of 82
per cent. of the women of this country
working for their living is an ugly rebuff

to the pretty platitudes about the home.
Whereas none but the most imbecile can
really imagine that the privilege of voting
for a member of Parliament will drive
a woman from her home. It may help
to keep her not only in her home as it
is, but to make it a healthier, happier,
heartier place to stay in than it often is
now. And this brings me to the equally
dreary apprehension expressed by some,
I am afraid, insincere people, that the
vote will lead to quarrels in the family.
"There were families in France," says
Mrs. Harrison, "where the *affaire Dreyfus*
could not be mentioned and," &c., &c., &c.
Quite so ; they did not wait for the vote
to find something to quarrel about. "The
wise mother will not hide her difference
of opinion, but she will not insist." I
have a marginal note to this which I
repeat : "What will the wise father do ?"
Further on, however, we are told : "If a
wife votes against [by which I suppose is
meant for a different candidate from] her
husband it will destroy her home influence
for ever." How fragile her influence is
supposed to be ! "Women must not be

afraid to proclaim afresh their belief in the supreme importance and beauty of the work of the humblest mother of a family where she is a brave, good woman." When I read this I felt a ribald inclination to exclaim : "*Are* we downhearted?" By all means let us go on "proclaiming" this ; I, for one, am "not afraid" to do so.

"We make bold to say," says Mrs. Harrison, "that the opinion of women in the past has been a national asset of the first importance." If this be true no other argument in favour of the suffrage is necessary ; give this "national asset" its full, direct, and rightful share in the representation of the members who control the affairs of their nation

Finally, Mrs. Harrison ends with these words: "It seems to us that in taking the vote women would be selling their birthright for a mess of pottage." That may be true. But it depends upon the relative value of the birthright and the pottage, as to whether it is worth while to do so. I imagine that there are some people who would be very sorry to exchange their pottage for any one else's birthright !

IX

THE PRESENT DISABILITIES OF
THE WOMEN OF ENGLAND

SINCE the days when John Stuart Mill
wrote his famous diatribe on the "Subjection of Women," a few of the grossest
injustices from which women suffered
have been removed. As a result women
have been complacently assured that at
present they have no grievances. But it
is not a paradox to say that the more
scope they have the more do the disabilities which still remain make themselves felt. Nor is it exaggeration to say
that in almost every department of life
artificial barriers exist which make it
impossible for women to compete on
terms of equality with their male fellow-
workers. This is assuming that every
human creature born into the world has
his or her sphere of utility. But this is
not recognised as a fact. Women are

regarded, and too often regard themselves, as drones, or as mere accessories to the utility, the convenience, or the comfort of males. It is this point of view wherein lies the initial error, and it is this which the pioneers of the "Woman's Movement" are trying gradually and strenuously to dissipate. Mr. Chesterton says of Mrs. Browning that she "contrived to assert, what still needs, but then urgently needed, assertion, the fact that womanliness, whether in life or poetry, was a positive thing, and not the negative of manliness."

It is difficult for those who have given much thought and consideration to this subject to conceive the apathy or intolerance with which this awakening of women is generally regarded. Mill's book, to which reference has been made, being casually mentioned in conversation the other day, I heard a normally intelligent well-educated man assume, not having read the book, and *not* in jest, that Mill had written *advocating* the subjection of women ! He no longer assumes this, but

the incident affords an illustration of the
strange ignorance that exists amongst
even thinking people of a movement
which has been making steady progress
during the last 100 years, has as advocates
some of the most distinguished persons of
this and the last centuries, and which
certainly no one can afford, nowadays, to
treat with contempt.

I have asserted above that in almost
every department in life women are handi-
capped in the race of life. And I am
going to try to substantiate that assertion.
Perhaps the only plane on which they
mix on an equality with men is on the
purely social plane. Here, I think, it is
fair to assume that in spite of Mrs.
Grundy, there is now a very fair equality
of treatment in matters relating to what is
commonly called "morals." Women who
have committed breaches in this respect
are treated with more leniency than
formerly, and men with less. It is due
to the unconscious influence of the
"Woman's Movement." But this partial
adjustment has not extended to the law.

DISABILITIES OF WOMEN

The divorce laws which enable a man to divorce his wife for committing an offence which he may commit a thousand times with impunity, so far as the law is concerned, are, as every one knows, egregiously unfair to women. Unless the view of a friend of mine be adopted, who complained bitterly of the injustice of a law that compelled him to ill-treat his wife before she had the right to get rid of him! As to the equity of the divorce laws, we are all familiar with the arguments, and they need not be entered into here; but what grounds of sanctity or sanity are there for the difference that exists in the lunacy law with regard to male and female lunatics?

What, too, can be more glaring than the inequality between men and women in the laws of descent or heredity? The male issue is favoured in every possible way. Why? Is it because women are stronger and in less need of material assistance? No; it is simply because men only, and not men and women, are responsible for the laws.

191

THE HUMAN WOMAN

The laws relating to libel and slander also "favour the male," a woman's reputation being a very much cheaper article in the eyes of legislators than a man's. Why it should be considered so is not obvious to the prejudiced female vision any more than it would be to a Parliamentary candidate if he happened to be soliciting the votes of the female portion of his electorate !

In *Contracts* the laws for men and women are unequal and generally unfair to women. A wife cannot bind her husband's estate, but a husband can bind all his wife's property not being her separate estate. A married woman cannot obtain the relief of the Bankruptcy Acts in respect of any antenuptial debt, even if she has separate property ; but a married woman on the death of her husband becomes liable for all her antenuptial debts to the extent of all her property. In some cases the benefit of prenuptial contracts made by the wife vests on marriage in the husband. A woman deserted by her husband must obtain from a police-magis-

trate a protection order protecting any
lawful earnings or property acquired by
her since the desertion. A wife living
apart from her husband cannot contract a
femme sole.

In *Litigation* a man would be entitled to
sue in the High Court without giving
security, a woman would not be allowed
to do so.

In the *Criminal law* it is an offence for
a woman to " solicit," but no such charge
can be preferred against a man, who can
only be proceeded against in some other
way : for obstruction, molestation, or
annoyance.

In *Company law* women are under disadvantages as compared to men for no
apparent reason beyond their sex. If a
married woman applies for shares in a
Company she may be subjected to humiliation by the directors requiring that the
husband shall become joint holder even if
the money be entirely her own.

The inequalities at present existing in
the laws relating to divorce, heredity,
lunacy, slander and libel, contracts, litiga-

tion, criminal and company law prove that
women are invariably at a disadvantage
when confronted with any of the difficulties of life. Mr. Cecil Chapman, the
most enlightened of our Police-magis-
trates, in a letter to the *Times* of July 23
this year, says—

" Those who administer the laws which
deal with questions of bastardy, desertion,
the separation of married people, solicita-
tion in the streets, the use of houses for
habitual prostitution, intemperance, not to
speak of other matters, like employment
in shops and factories or the education of
children, are daily and hourly impressed
with the conviction that these laws, whatever their merits may be, have been made
by men for the most part in their own
interests without due regard to the interests of women, who suffer in a much
greater degree than men the consequences
of irregular and difficult lives, but have not
been allowed to express their opinions in
legislation as to the best way of finding
a remedy. Man, who is their political
master, has chosen to have it in this way

and no other, and there is an end of the matter. That may be expedient, but nobody can reasonably say that it is just."

But these inequalities sink into insignificance compared with the disabilities that dog their footsteps in every movement of their lives from the cradle to the grave. I particularly desire not to deal in hyperbole, but I do not think that this contention shoots one inch above the mark. In their very education, where it is not openly and obviously in the boy's favour, which it generally is, there is an insidious difference operating almost invisibly but still considerably to the advantage of the male as against the female student. For, that many women are unconscious of the great force working against them does not prevent it from being a fact ; and, if it be a fact, from its having a damaging influence on women in particular, and on the race in general. But in the matter of University degrees the refusal to give equal recognition to women for equal achievement is so indefensible, that it has only to be mentioned to be shamefacedly admitted.

THE HUMAN WOMAN

If then, her so-called " education " completed, a woman desires employment of
any kind she is again confronted with
obstruction due solely to the fact of her
sex, which need disqualify her for none of
the situations open to her, nor for hundreds that are closed to her. And here
we arrive at that part of the subject under
consideration where women suffer the most
grievous injustices and where women's
demand for the Parliamentary franchise
receives its most insistent justification.
For if at this moment a Bill came into
force granting the franchise to women on
the same terms that men now vote, the
new voters would be about 90 per cent.
working-women. The Lancashire and
Cheshire Women Textile and other
Workers' Representation Committee collected the percentage of working-women
and other classes of women who would be
placed on the register in Nelson, Bolton,
Kirkby-Lonsdale, Barnsley, Leeds, Cambridge, and Darwen, and it was found that
the percentage varied from 100 per cent.
to 65 per cent., the greater number being

90 to 95 per cent. The condition of these working-women needs improvement. It has never been disputed that the bestowal of the suffrage on working-men improved their condition. The position of the women workers shows no corresponding improvement. Mr. Sidney Webb says in his " Labour in the Longest Reign " · " Women's wages for unskilled labour still gravitate pretty close to the subsistence level below which they can never have sunk for any length of time. Out of the four millions of women who are working for wages at the present time, a very large percentage must be earning practically no better subsistence than their grandmothers did." The deduction is obvious.

Now let it be remembered that the whole of the restrictions as to employment in factories and workshops are restrictions on the employment of women, young persons, and children only. Men are free to work what hours they choose. In this connection a very wide meaning is given in the Factory Act to the word " employment." It has been held to include a manageress,

who, in addition to her salary, takes a share in
the profits and is mistress of her own house.

It is impossible without going into the
subject at very great length to give a full list
of the restrictions under which women are
placed by these Factory Acts. But shortly it
may be said, that their hours are restricted ;
they must not work on Sunday, they must
not be continuously employed for more
than four and a half or five hours without
an interval of at least half-an-hour for a
meal ; they must not work inside and outside a factory on the same day ; if employed
inside a factory they must not take work
home in the evening ; and there is a general
rule that overtime is not allowed in textile
factories. No night employment to women
is allowed in textile factories. Women
are prohibited from cleaning mill gearing
machinery in a factory where the machinery
is in motion for the purpose of propelling
any part of the manufacturing machinery,
and must not work between the fixed and
traversing part of any self-acting machine
where the machine is in motion. There
are special regulations and exceptions as to
hours and holidays, overtime and meal time.

DISABILITIES OF WOMEN

The employment of women below ground
in mines is prohibited and their employment
restricted above ground. None of these
restrictions or provisions apply to men

Now while it is open to question as to
whether or not these restrictions act beneficially for women, or whether, if they be
just and wise restrictions, they should not
apply equally to men and women working
in the same trade, it cannot under any
stretch of the imagination be argued that
the male voters are more likely to judge
fairly, clearly, and unselfishly as to whether
these restrictions act beneficially for the
women, than the women-workers themselves.

The difference in the wages paid to men
and to women for the same work, admittedly, bears no relation to the difference
in the quality of the work done by men
and by women. " It is generally allowed,"
says Miss Roper, " that the low rate of
women's wages tends to bring down the
standard for both sexes, and is a constant
source of damage to the interests of all
workers." And it is not only in the
lowest grade of work that this inequality

in pay exists. The scale adopted by the Manchester Education Committee in 1903 gives as salaries for *Principal Teacher* :—

Masters (after five years' work) £135 (after fifteen years) £175
Mistresses ,, ,, ,, ,, 90 ,, ,, ,, 110

	Head-masters per unit.	Head mistresses per unit
For the first 300 scholars	4s. 0d.	2s 0d.
For the next 100 ,,	3s 0d	1s 6d.

Certified Assistants are paid

	Commencing Salaries.	Maximum
Men	£75	£140
Women. . . .	55	110

Pupil Teachers ·

	First Year	Second Year.	Third Year
Boys .	£22 10 0	£25	£27 10 0
Girls . .	12 0 0	15	18 0 0

The proportion of the salaries of men and women is the same throughout. "There is no attempt made to assert any inferiority on the part of the women-teachers," to quote Miss Roper again. "They pass the same examinations and are generally allowed to be as good teachers as men."

In the General Post Office also women are invariably paid less than men for precisely the same work.

Men, second division lower grade .	£70 to £250
Women, second class . .	65 to 80
Men, second division higher grade	250 to 350
Women, first class . .	85 to 110

DISABILITIES OF WOMEN

In the district offices and provinces :—

	Men	Women
First-class sorting clerks	. 40s. to 56s	18s. to 40s.
Second-class sorting clerks	. 28s to 35s	15s to 28s.

The pay provided by the London County Council for the work inaugurated by the Council's different departments shows the same inequality and inadequacy in the wages paid to their female *employées*.

Now so far from there being any obvious or good reason for this disproportional payment, it merely means that women have to work harder for what they earn than men. For the " weaker sex " are unable to command the leisure that adequate payment would give them, and have to use their spare time in the uncongenial employment of " making both ends meet." Instead of being able, as men are, to buy their clothing at reliable shops and to pay a price which guarantees the excellence and durability of their purchases, they have to skimp, to patch, and to contrive in order to turn themselves out in such a condition as will assure to them the continuance of their situation, and at the sacrifice of labour and worry for which they have no return. This applies to their food also. The nourishing necessary food that men are enabled by their better pay to command is beyond a working-woman's reach, and in addition to this " household work " is exacted from them over and above their regular occupation. In a word, " working-women " do two classes of work in the same day for about half the pay received by men for doing one class of work only. The thinking portion amongst the working-men by no means advocate this cruel disparity. " By treating women," says Mr. Keir Hardie, M.P., " I am speaking now from the working-class point of view —as equals, by conceding to them every concession which men claim for themselves the women will play the part of the equal, not only in regard to wages, but in all other matters appertaining to industrial life."

The Women's Trade Union League, admirable and indefatigable as is their work, is unable to obtain the concessions that are demanded for women in the name of equity and even common-sense Repeated resolutions have been passed calling upon the Home Secretary for a substantial increase in the number of women-inspectors, without effect. The number was and remains wholly inadequate. And this is a typical case of the apathy and indifference shown to the needs of the unenfranchised. Questions are asked over and over again in Parliament, by the friends of the League, vague answers, sometimes promises, are returned and— nothing is done.

It has been seen that in the profession of teaching, and of post-office clerkships, women fare no better than in the humbler walks of life, when their work comes into competition with the work where the male worker has established a secure footing, and where he endeavours to obtain a monopoly. Why, for instance, should women not be barristers, solicitors, accountants, or clerks in the numerous offices from which they are now excluded solely by reason of their sex ? In all the professions I have mentioned women have been known to train themselves, have passed the necessary examinations, fulfilled the necessary conditions, and have then been deliberately excluded on account of their sex. It would occupy far too much space to enumerate all the known or even the notorious cases, but the assertion will not be disputed by any one who takes the trouble to acknowledge facts. The act of acknowledging facts does not at first sight appear to involve much "trouble," but a great deal of trouble is taken to dispute, minimise, or ignore facts that would bear heavily on the unstable ground of the *status quo*. The opposition put forth by men is supported by various and opposite reasons. Sometimes it is ostensibly on women's account, sometimes it is frankly on selfish grounds : that men do not want women to "come swamping the professions." As if the world were in so perfect a condition that only a limited amount of work were necessary to "keep it going !" Whereas in truth if every unit put forth all its strength and virtue, ability and power in improving the world there would still be work left undone. It is a sign of the times that almost every modern novel touches however incidentally and lightly, but still touches on the question of woman's status. Mr. Anthony Hope in his last novel makes one of his characters say, in discussing the desirability of a certain lady as a wife whose prospective father-in-law objected to women who worked for their living: " If she married of course she wouldn't want the money, would she ? " Mr Hope's commentary is: " Any other end of a profession had not occurred to him, and his opinion [previously expressed] that active and public avocations were not ' unsexing ' to women was limited by the proviso that such employments must be necessary for bread and butter."

Now in reply to the constantly reiterated assertion of the anti-suffragists that the extension of the franchise to women would not affect their economic position, we have the lately established fact that, in view of a prospective election in Norway, the wages of female Government *employées* in the post and telegraph offices have been raised. So averse are our opponents from conceding any point which they are forced to admit controverts the assertions that they have been in the habit of making, that when this fact of the promise of increased pay was made in an argument, I heard it denounced as an instance of the demoralisation likely to ensue from women forming a portion of the electorate ! This promise held out before a general election was, I was told, "a glaring instance of bribery and corruption."

Now, that this prospect of better payment should be justly regarded as a bribe presupposes two things. First, that the pay of these women had not hitherto been inadequate, and, secondly, that a sense of justice was wholly absent in those from whom the proposal emanated ; but who were, nevertheless, eminently fitted, in sole virtue of their sex, to conduct the affairs of their nation. If both these conditions could be established, it merely shows woeful want of foresight on the part of those willing to corrupt what, after all, would be a very small proportion of the electorate. If the women whose wages the existing Ministry stated its intention of raising considered themselves, and were considered by their fellow-electors, amply paid already, the repayment by them of a few votes for this injustice to the rest of the community would not compensate for the loss of other votes, both from women who did not benefit and from the men who would also be affected by this act of injustice. If, however, the post-office officials were underpaid, why should the announcement that this grievance would be remedied be considered in the light of a "bribe" because it was made previous to an election? And why should the women be made responsible? It is quite possible that had women not been in possession of a vote this grievance, amongst many others, might, and very likely would, have been left unredressed; but this merely emphasises the indisputable fact that the grievances of those who are represented receive the attention that the grievances of the unrepresented do not receive. But to stigmatise the promise of such legislation as bribery is to travesty all representative government and to relegate all electoral programmes to the lowest level of sale and barter. A few weeks ago the following paragraph in a London newspaper bearing on this subject attracted my attention.

"WOMEN AND MEN IN THE POST OFFICE

"The announcement that woman clerks of the Established Civil Service employed in the General Post Office are in future to receive a commencing salary of £65 per annum *will not arouse any serious criticism.* But, the London correspondent of the *Manchester Guardian* states, *it is exciting discontent amongst another section of the Civil Service,* the male assistant clerks, who begin at £55 only, and receive an annual increment of but £2, 10s. These have quite as good qualifications as the average woman clerk, and do arduous if not re-

sponsible work. *That they should be paid
not only less than women*, but at a rate
lower than that allowed by the Postmaster-
General for unskilled labourers, is a matter
that certainly seems to demand inquiry,
and the whole case of this class of Civil
servant is to be brought before the
House of Commons at an early opportunity."

The three sentences that I have italicised are instructive. Firstly, the writer
of the paragraph generously suggests that
the fact that women's work is to receive
more adequate payment "will not arouse
any serious criticism"! Secondly, the
paragraph goes on to say that nevertheless this increased pay to women "*is
exciting discontent*" amongst the men,
and thirdly, the fact that they should
be paid less than women "is a matter
that certainly seems to demand inquiry,"
even though the inference is clear that
although they have " quite as good qualifications as the *average* woman clerk "
the work of those who feel themselves
aggrieved is, if arduous, *not* so responsible

as the work of the women whose salaries have been raised.

The reasoning of anti-suffragists is seldom above the level of the arguments used on the occasion to which I have referred, anent bribery, and is a good illustration of the old adage that any stick is good enough to beat a dog with.

One prominent member of this new Anti-Suffrage League admitted to me in the course of conversation that he had no reasons against extending the Parliamentary vote to women, but he had, he said, a deep-rooted, and indeed ineradicable, prejudice—"and prejudice," he added, "held with the fervour with which this prejudice holds me is far stronger than any reason." This, however, was a man. There are some women who try to justify their prejudice with some attempt to advance what they regard as reasons. But most of these reasons are based on the assumption that the present state of society as regards the established relation of the sexes is natural, and consequently unalterable. Now, any one with an elementary knowledge of sociology in its historic and prehistoric aspect knows that the established basis of society as it exists in the civilised world at the present day is strangely different from the basis upon which various societies existed in some earlier stages of civilisation. The human race went through many stages, backwards and forwards, till it reached its present by no means stable or unalterable condition. The male of the race from being originally merely the fertiliser became (with the recognition of his joint parenthood, which, like the males in the lower animal world, he "in the beginning" was entirely unconscious of) the hunter, the producer, and eventually the breadwinner.[1] Now, most anti-suffrage arguments are based on the assumption that the male is still the only producer and breadwinner, whereas this is very far from being the case. When it is realised that of the adult female population of this country 82 per cent. are wage-earners it will be seen that to base any argument on the assumption that on

[1] See pp 104, 105.

men alone falls the whole responsibility as the producers and supporters of the race such an argument must necessarily be, to use merely the mildest form of condemnation, very unsound.

It is not disputed that legislative proposals are instigated by the wishes, supposed or expressed, of the people who are represented in the legislative assemblies, neither is it disputed that laws are enacted directly concerning the female portion of the community. Moreover, it has been shown that the establishment of Women's Suffrage in Norway produces proposals directly and favourably influencing the condition of women working under the pay of the Government. But it may be argued that this improvement would have taken place had women remained voteless. So little, however, is this believed that proposed legislation obviously beneficial to certain classes of voters is immediately called bribery by some high-minded, disinterested spectators of the phenomenon. Both views, therefore, as they directly contradict each other, cannot be correct, and the simple explanation that the vote is an instrument that has been proved to be beneficial to working-men, and could not fail also to benefit working-women, must be met by our opponents, and satisfactory reasons for withholding this valuable instrument be given, or they stand convicted of wanton injustice.

I have read all the "literature" produced by this new Anti-Suffrage League, and I maintain that not one single satisfactory reason is forthcoming. Mrs. Humphry Ward, whom, I suppose, we must consider their most able spokeswoman, is willing to admit that there are and always will be "matters before Parliament which specially concern women," that these matters should be "clearly and effectively expressed" as "these things" [not specified] "rightly belong to women as their share in the public life and work of England." She suggests that "some further machinery should be devised" to obtain this clear and effective expression of opinion by bringing *women* into "consultative rela-

tion with the Home Office and Local
Government Board." Now in formulat-
ing this opinion Mrs. Ward is guilty
of a species of subconscious arrogance.
It is not the women who are primarily
concerned by the legislation likely to
affect their lives and work who are to
be placed in this consultative relationship
with the offices she names, but a limited
number of unrepresented and unrepresen-
tative women who are willing to be the
self-constituted mouthpiece of the women
whose interests they are supposed to
undertake to serve. But as Mr. Eliot,
a Rhodes Scholar, writing to the *Times*
in answer to one of Mrs. Ward's letters
justly points out. "Women's public work
outside Parliaments, even on Local
Government Boards, if unaccompanied
by representation in Parliament, can
never rise above amateur grade, and will
never be valued at any other standard
by responsible people."

If this suggested machinery were in-
stituted, these consulting and consulted
ladies might have their sense of import-

ance and their vanity agreeably tickled ; but their contribution to effective legislation would be *nil*.

If the amount of spasmodic attention this "consultative relationship" would involve *is* necessary to women's interests, it will be difficult to prove why women's demand for representation on the same terms as it is or may be conceded to men should not be granted. If, however, the aforesaid amount of attention is adequate to the claims of the female portion of the population, it will be equally difficult to show why more should be conceded to the male portion thereof.

Now, if the reasons that Shakespeare put into the mouth of Katherine, the tamed shrew, for her willingness to obey her tyrant were valid on the ground that the man "commits his body to painful labour, both by sea and land, to watch the night in storm, the day in cold," while woman lies "warm at home, secure and safe," then "love, fair looks, and true obedience" were indeed "too little payment for so great a debt."

THE HUMAN WOMAN

But, unfortunately, this aspect of women is wholly untrue, in view of this fact that 82 per cent of the women of this country actually work for their living, while the remaining 18 per cent. mostly " earn their keep " by service of some kind, either by their unpaid work in the home or by serving their communities on public bodies. Their work, then, has a right to acknowledgment by direct representation, whereas both men and women who argue against the extension of the franchise to women not only ignore women's contributions to the State in actual labour and general thought, but speak of the debt of gratitude that women owe to men as being so great that they should be content to leave all legislation in their hands. This is to ignore the facts of life.

Then, again, there is a mistaken idea that women's work conflicts with men's, that women would interfere with and appropriate work better done by men. I believe, on the contrary, that with the amalgamation of the male and female element in public life there would come eventually a total readjustment of the world's work infinitely to the advantage of the community as a whole. Even now women who wish to do work better suited to men are rare, as rare as the men one occasionally hears of who, even when a woman is in the house, assume the whole management thereof. The man does this either from want of another and more useful occupation, or through petty economy and mistrust of the powers of the person who ought to do it, or through overestimating the importance of the gratification of his appetite, which he thinks his culinary judgment is better able to minister to, than his wife's. But these men are as rare as the women who from deliberate choice undertake work admittedly better done by men.

The stupendous mistake that has been made up to now is in supposing that it is men's judgment only that should decide these questions, and hence the hopeless state of unravelled misery existing in the world side by side with all the wealth and wonders of the age.

THE HUMAN WOMAN

If we examine the condition of the working classes after years and years of male legislation, what a hideous set of conditions we find. With a decrease in the general death-rate, infant mortality is almost at a stand-still. What are the causes of this? Intemperance, bad housing, poverty, and the cruel struggle for existence among the poorer classes. And yet we spend over £22,000,000 annually on the education of these very people. Surely there is something wrong somewhere! What is it, that we, seeing this condition of things at our very door have, as women, to be so grateful for in male legislation? "Women's concern is the home" is the phrase we have unceasingly dinned into our ears. It is the homes where these deplorable conditions exist, and these homes alone, that are affected by legislation, and it is in this necessary remedial legislation that women's co-operation is absolutely essential if any real improvement is to be effected.

Not to be able to see this appears to me to be the most petrified blindness; and the women who applaud men for their refusal to accept women's co-operation seem to me to be altogether unworthy of their place in creation. Whatever may be their social position the avowed anti-suffrage women belong to the parasite class. They may vaunt their own intelligence, their own independence, and their own achievements, whether as writers, organisers, explorers, or travellers, but the parasite germ clings to their blood, and taints the very air they breathe : being unconscious of it they make no effort to shake it off. They do not desire, they cannot even imagine truer freedom either for themselves or their fellow-women. They see no disgrace in preferring to remain in their present unenfranchised condition. They suffer no inconvenience themselves from their restricted outlook on life, it is therefore inconceivable to them that other women should be able to have a wider, higher, more far-reaching and truer view, than the one they are able to grasp. Whether they realise the fact or not they are parasites, and consciously or unconsciously they resent the attitude adopted by the women whose thoughts are to them a closed book. They sneer at the hopes held out by those who would counteract their evil influence: they pretend that we see in the vote the end-all and be-all of existence. It is false. We see in its refusal to women a temporary and futile but sinister bar to the rightful heritage of all mankind, and to that fuller, freer life where there shall ultimately be neither votes nor voters, neither parties nor partizans, but human men and human women working together for the common good of their common humanity. In the process of evolution the hour has struck when this great reform has become necessary to the salvation of this nation; when to delay it is a danger. Retributive justice is crying out to her, " Put your house in order." There are women who have heard that cry, and who are asking to be allowed to help. We have reason to believe that this offer of help will not be again and indefinitely refused.

INDEX

INDEX

INDEX

223

INDEX

INDEX

INDEX

INDEX

227

INDEX

Printed by BALLANTYNE, HANSON & CO.
Edinburgh & London